D1527040

WHEN THE HEART
IS LONELY

WHEN THE HEART
IS LONELY

INEZ SPENCE

BAKER BOOK HOUSE
Grand Rapids, Michigan

*To my daughters-in-law, Donna and Phoebe,
who have made being a mother-in-law such
a happy experience.*

Contents

*I have noticed that folks are gen-
erally about as happy as they have
made up their minds to be.*

— Unknown

Chapter 1

Two for a Penny

It promised to be another grey, drizzly day. Spring, all dressed up in soft sunshine, had given a teasing smile then flitted away with only a vague promise to return. With a disappointed grimace Melissa Nelson turned from her window. Reluctantly she looked at the sink filled with unwashed dishes.

"I know you're there," she muttered. "I know the whole tiresome routine. After you are put away I take my unenthusiastic steps upstairs to restore order to the bedrooms my rowdy sons and teen-age daughter left so blithely behind them. Then comes the laundry with time wedged in for countless tasks — shopping for groceries, planning dinner, and greeting my returning family with a smiling face."

She gave a last look out of the window. A trio of tiny sparrows balanced lightly on a slender twig as the strong wind swung them to and fro.

"Why couldn't you have been a cardinal wearing a gay spring outfit?" she scolded. "At least that would be a flash of color in all this grey. Even a perky robin would help. But only sparrows to match the drabness! I've never really thought about sparrows before, yet I do remember that they are mentioned in the Bible."

Like a persistent little ache the picture of the three sparrows outside her window nagged her thinking. Taking the Bible from its place, she began to search. In the Book of Matthew she found the reference. With interest she read:

> Are not two sparrows sold for a penny? And yet not one of them will fall to the ground without your Father's leave and notice.
>
> But even the very hairs of your head are all numbered.
>
> Fear not, then: you are of more value than many sparrows.
>
> — Matthew 10:29-31 (Amplified Version)

"Two sparrows for a penny," Melissa repeated to herself. "Each one worth only one-half cent. The little I know about sparrows is certainly not to their credit. Their reputation is quite unsavory. Doesn't it seem strange that God would use them to illustrate His love and watchcare?"

That evening at dinner Melissa surprised her family by asking, "What do you know about sparrows?" Their lack of knowledge matched her own so the next day when her neighbor ran in to chat, Melissa asked, "Marge, what do you know about sparrows?"

"Sparrows?" Marge echoed. "Really nothing; why?"

"Oh, I just wondered," Melissa answered. "They are so common it surprised me that I knew so little about them."

That afternoon Melissa brought home a bird book

from the library and began to search for the answer to her question — "Why would God speak with such concern of a sparrow valued at only two for a penny?"

They are such ordinary little birds. Devoid of lovely coloring, their brown-black top feathers seem to be dimmed by the off-white of their underparts. Even the tail feathers are a brownish grey. No scarlet hat — no bright crown — just uninteresting brown and black and dirty white. Surely of all the birds, the sparrow is among the least attractive.

Often their nests are found on the ground in fields or woods, hidden by sheltering tussocks of grass. Sometimes their nests are found in bushes or small trees. Their eggs are also dull — a pale greenish color with spots of reddish brown and lavender.

Melissa was surprised to find that the sparrow is really a foreigner. Eight pairs of sparrows were brought over from England in 1850. They multiplied rapidly, fighting valiantly for survival. Being winter birds they are well established in the best nesting places and know where the best feeding places are to be found before the summer birds arrive.

Their unclean habits have made them disliked and accusations against the sparrow are plentiful. Although the Biological Bureau of Birds credits the English sparrow with destroying certain insect pests, it also finds them guilty of destroying fruit, buds, flowers, and young vegetables. And the large amount of wheat they consume is a great loss to our country each year.

Even though these dubious qualities of this common bird added to Melissa's questioning rather than clarified why God should be so concerned with it, she continued her study. She had never before heard of the Vesper Sparrow. Its name intrigued her. The shyest of its kind, its simple little song is like an evening prayer of thanksgiving. Although it sings also in the daytime, the soft darkness of night calls forth a litany of praise with a violin-like quality. In its quiet way the Vesper Sparrow serves the farmer well by consuming beetles and grasshoppers and many other enemies of the farmer's crop.

Melissa read about the many kinds of sparrows, each with its individual characteristics. To her surprise she learned that whether one lives in the east or on the western coast, by the ocean side or on the plains, the sparrow is there. It is an ever present reminder that God watches over His own.

She closed the book and sat lost in thought. She was an attractive woman in her early thirties, but her blue eyes looked cloudy with questions as she again thought of the three little sparrows swinging on the tree branch just outside her window. She still felt depressed — her commonplace duties seemed so monotonous, so meaningless. She felt her life was so lacking in importance, so overwhelmed with mundane things. A rebellious kind of loneliness depressed her. It was as if she were being cheated. All the exciting things seemed to be passing her by.

"And I even look as dowdy as a sparrow," she told herself.

Melissa smiled at her own thoughts then turned back to her question — Why did God choose a sparrow to illustrate His love and watchcare over His children?

"What have I learned about sparrows that can explain it?" she asked herself. "They are of such little value," she reasoned. "Two could be bought for a penny. There may be a lesson in *that*. What really makes a life one of value? It isn't prestige or riches —

or even achievement. True, the world may applaud, but a life has no eternal value without Christ. It is a miracle of divine love that He can find in us qualities of value. Yet He loves us and is mindful of everything that touches our lives. I may not be an important person as the world counts importance, but I am important to Christ and to my family."

Melissa realized she was developing a feeling of kinship to these small feathered creatures. She thought of the Ipswich Sparrow. Skulking in beach grass near the ocean it offered no appreciable help to man — a timid little bird with no song.

"Rather a sad little bird," Melissa decided. "Afraid, and with no lilting tones of courage to sing to the world. And about us are human hearts that have no song — that is even sadder."

But the Lark Sparrow, she recalled, is loved for its sweet music. Gay and happy, it can be heard almost continuously. Surely it must have to struggle to survive, yet it gives forth a joyous melody. How like people. Some find no joy, no bursts of praise, no looking beyond the problem to the One who can give the solution. Others, with burdens heavy to bear, look up and find strength to give cheer to others about them.

Melissa arose from her chair and walked to the window.

"I think I have found the answer to my question," she spoke aloud. "One thing I must never forget. It is this. The insignificant sparrow shows the way to the best feeder boxes. By following the sparrows the newcomers find the food placed there for their need by friendly hands. Perhaps this is the most important thing to remember. In the everydayness of our lives lies the opportunity to help others find the satisfaction and security that is found only through relationship with Christ. And how better could He have told us that even the least soul is important to Him?"

Melissa was right. Abraham Lincoln once said that God must have loved the common people because He made so many of them. Most of us are ordinary people, living ordinary lives and meeting ordinary life situations.

Sorrow, losses, heartache, financial problems, family difficulties touch most lives during the years. Discouragement, worry, anxiety, fear — all are common foes. How we meet them is the important thing. Sometimes it helps to learn about the experiences of others. The true stories told in the following pages are hopefully meant to bring encouragement and help.

Seldom can the heart be lonely,
If it seek a lonelier still;
Self-forgetting, seeking only
Emptier cups of love to fill.
　　　　　　　— FRANCES RIDLEY HAVERGAL

Chapter 2

A New Assignment in Living

The tearoom was crowded. Slipping into a chair at a small table I noticed two women seated near me — smartly coiffured, a flash of lipstick worn like a badge of courage, eyes tired and unhappy.

I listened as they talked. "I dread each day," one was saying. "Each new day. And the nights are even worse. No one understands what it means to be suddenly left alone. My whole life has crumpled beneath me. There just doesn't seem to be anything left."

As I listened, I remembered. I understood her words. I knew about the numbing pain; I knew about those desolate hours of the night that turned into another desolate day. I *knew.*

"If only I could tell them," I thought. "If I could say, 'Pardon me, please, but may I tell you what I have learned from sorrow?'"

I couldn't. I remembered how slow I had been in learning the lesson of acceptance. Life seemed so bleak and courage almost too weak to put forth the effort.

No, I couldn't intrude upon these women but I could silently pray:

"Lord Jesus, help these lonely hearts to find You. To know that You care, that You share the grief. To feel Your healing touch upon the throbbing pain. To find again direction and meaning in living."

My sorrow is no longer new. But etched deep in my memory are those first days of heartache and loss. Within a few terrifying moments I lost my companion. Without warning my whole life was changed. Our two stalwart sons came quickly to steady me with their strength and love. There were the kindnesses of wonderful friends, the expressions of sympathy from near strangers. Yet like a throbbing beat that could not stop, I heard the words over and over in my heart — "Alone-alone-alone."

Like a nightmare from which there was no awakening, those first days dragged their endless hours slowly away. Wise sons quietly assumed that meals would be served at the regular hours and household tasks performed as usual. Gradually my thoughts began to fall into place and I faced the question, "What do I do now?"

The memory of that last day I spent with my sons is like a soft light in a darkened room. Both boys were leaving, the older to his work in Mexico, the younger for his senior year in college with medical school ahead. Early that morning I was alone with my firstborn.

"I want to talk with you, Mother," he said. "We wish that we could be near you but we know that you will face this new life with true courage. You will find interests, worthwhile interests, that will bring satisfaction, even happiness.

"Right now, Mother, these next few weeks, is the

danger time. Everyone is going to be very kind and sympathetic. Be careful to accept it sparingly. Self-pity can smother every effort to be confident and strong. It cripples initiative — stifles healing laughter — distorts truth — blinds one to the good things about you — keeps you from seeing the needs of others. Self-pity can destroy its victims. Mother, your words, the tone of your voice, your attitude for the next few weeks will set the pattern for the rest of your life."

"Have you thought me complaining or childish?" I asked.

"No," he assured me. "No, we are proud of you. But you know that you have forfeited the right to grieve as many others may."

"What do you mean?" I demanded.

He smiled as he answered, "Why, Mother, you have taught others that Christ can meet every need."

And out of the secure, happy past, I heard my own words assuring others, "The Lord Jesus never puts upon His child any burden without giving the strength to bear it. For every heartwound He pours the healing oil of His love and care. In many ways He reveals the closeness of His presence, and His nearness brings comfort and help. He puts new courage in the heart and He gives us the will to go on.

"A child of God *may* ask, 'What do You want me to do, Lord? Where do You want me to serve?' But the Christian should *not* ask, 'Why, Lord, have You allowed this to happen to me? Why, Lord, why?'

"Learning to trust when you cannot understand His reasons; learning to accept without questioning His way and His goodness; learning to yield to His will without complaining — this is the Christian's part."

I remembered the words. I believed them. Now was

17

the time to prove them. Somehow, facing the words that I had given to others in their times of sorrow stimulated my own faith. My heart reached out to receive the help I needed to make them a reality now in my own life.

Later that morning my son called me from downtown.

"How is my favorite girl?" he asked me.

And I answered, "Smarting but surviving. You were very wise, my dear, and I thank you."

As I turned from the telephone I knew that somehow I had taken a short step in the right direction. I had faced self-pity. In my heart I had wanted to hold it close. But I had seen it in the clear light of a new morning and I knew it for the enemy it is.

Way into the late, late hours that night we talked together, the three of us. Funny little family happenings were recalled. Memories were relived and in the sharing of happy times our sorrow was softened.

" 'Alone' is the saddest word in our language," I told them.

Quickly they answered, "No, Mother. There is a word that is far sadder. That word is 'fear.' You are not afraid. Not you, who have taught us faith and courage."

"I will not be afraid," I promised.

But when nighttime came in those first months alone, fear came also. Strange sounds, fancied or real, the disturbing quietness, all became things to dread. Nights seemed endless — too tired to think clearly, too tense to sleep. And each day was clouded with the dread of evening darkness.

Nagging, disturbing thoughts tugged for attention. Gentle reminders stirred my heart.

"This is not the way to heart rest and trust," they prodded my dull thinking. "Why don't you really try trusting in God's love and watchcare?"

That night as I turned the lock in the door I spoke aloud, "Even as I lock the door for safety, I will lock fear from my heart. I do have faith in Christ to take care of me. I will not allow fear to dishonor that trust."

Turning from the door I knew that I had taken another short step in the right direction.

There is nothing unusual about being lonely, I discovered. Neither is it limited to those who have lost their companions. A wedding ring is no insurance against loneliness, for some of the loneliest hearts are tied by a marriage vow.

Young hearts can know its torture. Wanting desperately to be accepted by their peers but feeling left out, unwanted — this is a dismal, lonely experience. Shy natures, sometimes thought to be unfriendly, know their own special brand of loneliness. The blight of loneliness has left its ugly mark on the lives of little children, hungry for love and security. Mature hearts are as vulnerable as the young or very old. No, there is nothing unusual about being lonely. But it must never be allowed to possess you — although it will try.

My story is very homemade and simple. There is nothing uncommon about being a woman alone in this land of ours. There are so many of us. Loneliness plays no favorites. In my work I have met lonely hearts of all ages and walks of life. Sometimes in the sharing of experiences there is encouragement and help.

I know many lonely women. Some go through the motions of daily living but within them is a numbing need that they do not know how to meet. I know others, many others, who have used their loneliness as steps reaching up to find new friends, helpful service, and a satisfying life.

It is easier to recognize God's part in the bitter experiences that come to us when we can look back without tears or heartbreak. Then we find that they gave us our sweetest times of prayer and the deepest lessons in trusting. They taught us the reality of His presence and the unfailing help that is found in His Word.

A long time ago I read the story of a little songbird. From its cage it enjoyed the bright sunshine and its beloved master's face, and it sang from sheer joy. Then the master sought to teach the little songster a new song. It would warble a note of it here, a measure there, then merrily resume a song of its own.

Gently the master covered the cage. Shut out were its merry companions, the beauty of sunshine, the master's face. Hidden away, the little bird heard the lesson notes. Gradually, in the loneliness of darkness, the tiny singer learned the new song, note by note. When its heart was filled with the new melody, the master uncovered the cage and out into God's glorious, sunshiny world went the new song.

Sometimes it takes sorrow and loneliness to make us aware of a lesson the Master would teach us. So occupied are we with our busy lives — personal interests, careers, plans, *things* — that our ears fail to hear the new notes. Only when sorrow covers the heart and we reach out in utter loneliness to the Master are we aware of the new song. It is a song of acceptance and submission. It is a song of faith. It is a song to give to others. It sings of a quiet confidence that the Master taught us in love and compassion. It is a song that lonely hearts about us need to hear.

It was Robert Louis Stevenson who said "In every

part and corner of our life, to lose one's self is to be the gainer, to forget one's self is to be happy."

Noble words! But how does one put them into practice? Forgetting one's self is the hardest task one can undertake. Forget self — when you are conscious only of its wearying pain, its demand for relief? Forget self — when loneliness wraps you in a grey blanket of despondency? Forget self? — How?

Have you tried substitution? It means that if something has been taken from you there is something else to fill the void. If self points to its own sorrow, then turn its eyes in compassion to another carrying a heavier burden than yours. If self wrings its hands in despair over loss of security, stretch out its hands to help one who has even less. If self shrivels in loneliness, cover it with friendliness and send it out to meet another's need of a friend.

These are not new truths. Wiser ones before us have proven their worth. In my first weeks alone they seemed like hands outstretched to help me but never quite close enough for me to grasp and hold them. I was desperately trying to hold familiar objects close — caring for a home that had turned into a house. Thinking — seeking — praying.

Over and over I heard one word. Old friends wanting only to help me told me often, "Things will be better for you when you have learned to adjust to your new way of living. But adjusting takes time and you must be patient. Adjustment is not easy for you but it will come in time."

Adjust! Adjust! Adjust!

I came to dread the very sound of the word, then I came to hate it. Slowly I was learning many lessons.

I found that there is a great difference between filling the hours to make the days endurable and finding a challenging motive to make the days worthwhile. I learned that no one ever jumps full-grown into adjustment or acceptance. Lessons are learned step by step. Each day brings its own conflicts and struggles. There was for me no lasting release from the loneliness. That had to come through persistent and determined effort. There is no magic way to find it. Each heart must find it for itself.

One night I knelt to pray. Very honestly I told the Lord my true feelings.

"I know, Lord Jesus, what I have to do. My heart is neither questioning nor resentful. The sorrow that You have sent me, I accept. But, please, Lord, give me a substitute word for that word 'adjust.' I cannot explain my feelings concerning it, I can only admit them. Give me something, please, that will be meaningful to me."

Quietly I waited. Long years ago I had learned that God meets the honest heart. Then, softly and clearly, came the words to my mind:

"A new assignment in living."

"Thank You, dear Lord," I cried. "Thank You so much. I accept the new assignment. I will not try to hide behind the door that You have shut. I will step out and face, without fear, the new door that You have opened."

Morning came. Like the words of a comforting hymn my heart sang the words — "A new assignment in living!"

And, that day I knew that I had taken a big step in the right direction.

I never knew a night so black
Light failed to follow in its track.
I never knew a storm so grey
It failed to have its clearing day.
I never knew such bleak despair
That there was not a rift, some-
where.
I never knew an hour so drear
Love could not fill it full of cheer.
— UNKNOWN

Chapter 3

The Person I Live With

How does one begin a new assignment in living? Where does one start? What preparation is necessary?

These were questions that my heart was asking. Nothing had changed, really. Aloneness was still new and acutely painful. That newfound courage to be unafraid stood on wobbly legs, ready to desert me completely, or to collapse when needed the most. But it never completely left me. That decision to commit all fear to Christ stiffened my efforts to put that decision into practice. Gradually I gained ground and the flicker of courage grew stronger with the passing days. There came the assurance that life, in a different way, could have new purpose and meaning.

Without tears and with a quieted heart I went often in prayer to talk it over with the Lord Jesus.

"Decrease my interest in every line that You are not choosing for me," I prayed. "And increase my interest in the direction that You are leading me."

Outwardly nothing happened. Weeks passed by and I was still waiting. It is so easy to wait *on* God with our requests — it is so hard to wait *for* God to bring things to pass.

Two verses became my constant companions. So often did I turn to them that my Bible opened naturally to the well read pages.

"Commit thy way unto the Lord, trust also in him and he shall bring it to pass" (Psalm 37:5).

"Rest in the Lord and wait patiently for him" (Psalm 37:7).

Commit — trust — rest — wait. These are the steps in divine order. God added one word, an adverb, describing how we are to wait — *patiently.* That is the secret and not an easy one to learn. Impulsive decisions and hasty actions only delay God's working. So does a fretful, impatient spirit. Slowly I was learning to wait, yet with expectation. A small glow of excitement began to color the days.

Evening hours were the hardest to accept. Day turning into night and no one coming home to me. Like a "five o'clock shadow" it would settle over me in intense and draining loneliness. The temptation was strong to become careless in preparing my meals. Gracious living didn't seem important when there was no one with whom to share it. Then self-discipline came to my rescue.

"I am a person," I reasoned with myself. "I must like and respect the person I live with. Graciousness and good manners make me a more pleasant companion if only to myself. Neither must my mind grow stagnant. Think of the dullness of living with a person whose mind has accepted early retirement!"

It was a victory, if only a small one. Carefully I set the table. At times a favorite piece of china seemed almost to smile at me in approval.

Substitute attempts? Yes, but a good substitute has something worthwhile to offer. Small niceties and careful grooming have a way of saluting one's self-respect. It helps. I found old friends waiting for me in the wonderful world of books and I made friends with new ones. Life was taking on a new pattern as I waited for God's leading.

Am I ready? Am I qualified for a new assignment in living? What character qualities do I need the most? These questions were always with me.

Friends had stopped in one evening for a short visit. It had been a pleasant evening and my heart was grateful for the blessing of friendships. Then my thoughts drifted back to my questions. All at once I remembered someone I had once known who had found the right answers. Someone I had known in my senior year at school. Memories came back in detail.

It was on a Friday morning. Weekend plans had tantalized our wandering thoughts as we sat through the student assembly session. Young legs ached to hurry on their eager ways; young eyes roved over the straight rows seeking out kindred spirits. And young hearts sang in the unison of youth, in the sheer joy of being alive and the thoughts of the free weekend ahead. On droned the dean's announcements. Then our lagging minds were caught by the quiet tones of the school president.

"Students," he began, "I wish to make a special announcement. Next Monday Professor Carlton Gleason joins our faculty. We are privileged to have him. His brilliant mind will challenge your thinking. His personality will win your admiration and liking." He paused, then finished slowly and clearly. "His handicap will demonstrate courage in its highest form."

An early Monday class had dragged me sleepy-eyed down the long halls. A new week lay ahead. Quickly I slipped into my front seat, then I looked in shocked surprise at the man facing the class. I had forgotten the president's announcement. What had he said? New professor. Handicap.

The eyes of the new teacher caught mine. A friendly smile lighted his pale face as he said, "Good morning."

"How are you?" I murmured.

A voice vibrant and strong replied, "I am cheerful — hopeful — optimistic — persevering — and determined."

In surprise the class listened, wondering and curious. Professor Gleason appeared to be in his early thirties. Seated in his wheelchair he looked oddly out of place in a classroom. His withered legs hung limply down, no longer than a very young child's. His finely shaped head seemed large for the frail shoulders. His thin face showed unmistakable traces of fatigue and physical weakness. Slender hands rested quietly on the arms of his chair — somehow one felt that they were strong hands and their owner a strong man.

All through that day the halls buzzed with the question, "Have you seen the new professor?"

Students, passing the new teacher, smiled and politely asked, "How are you?" They waited for his reply, "I am cheerful — hopeful — optimistic — persevering — and determined."

A week later a notice appeared on the bulletin boards: "Professor Gleason will lecture Friday night in King Hall. His subject is 'Growing Tall.'"

Word leaked out that Professor Gleason would be telling the story of his own life. That night King Hall was filled with interested and curious students.

Very simply Carlton Gleason told the story of his handicap and the long, hard battle to overcome the tremendous odds. Born in an eastern city, his active little body was stricken with polio at the age of three years. That dread disease left him paralyzed from his waist down, doomed to spend his life in a wheelchair.

He watched from the windows as his brothers played ball. Wistfully he would look at his withered legs and realize that he was different from other boys. On warm, sunny days his mother would wheel him out on the large front porch. From there he watched with envious eyes as school children skipped happily by.

Birthdays came and Carlton was ten. Then one day it happened. That morning the birds did not sing any sweeter to the little boy as he sat quietly watching the busy street. Neither did the sun shine any brighter. His heart did not whisper that a wonderful thing was about to happen to him. But it did.

Down the street came a man in a blue uniform. Over his shoulder hung a heavy leather bag. He came up the steps and smiled at the sober-eyed little boy.

"Hello," he said. "I am your new postman. I have a feeling that you and I are going to be friends."

And so it began. Each morning Carlton watched for his new friend. Then one day the postman said, "Carlton you are growing into a fine boy. God has given you a quick, fine mind. You are going to grow tall, little friend, very tall. Perhaps your body must always be smaller than you might wish, but your spirit and your mind are going to be tall and strong.

"Let us begin today. I am going to give you a word

27

to tuck in your heart and learn its meaning. That word is *cheerful*. It means being glad that you are alive with a family that loves you very much. It means knowing that you can never do many things that other boys do, yet being happy for the many things you can do and do well. It means making those about you happy, too."

So the game grew. "How are you today?" the postman would ask. Proudly Carlton would answer, "I am cheerful."

Soon the word *hopeful* was added.

"Carlton," his friend said, "you are going to study hard. You must go to college and one day you will be a fine teacher. You must never lose your hope, no matter how difficult it may be. Aim high, work hard, and your hopes will come true."

Over the months other words were learned. Words that directed and spurred the young boy on to believe that he had something to give to the world.

"How are you, Carlton?" came the daily question.

Eagerly came the answer, "I am cheerful — hopeful — optimistic — persevering — and determined."

Moving his chair closer to his audience, the young professor had concluded his story.

"It isn't the misfortune that comes to you that is important. It isn't the unhappy circumstances that face you. It isn't sorrow, loss, loneliness, disappointments, or even failure. The important thing is your attitude toward your problems."

Strange how the words of my teacher came back to me now so clearly. I needed them. In them I found the answer to my questions. These character qualities would fit me for the new assignment in living.

A cheerful spirit can be cultivated. Not a false face worn when others are there to see, but cheerfulness that comes from the heart. Do you remember the words that Christ spoke to Paul? Trouble as black as the night engulfed the apostle. Enemies were seeking his life. Beatings — imprisonment — hatred — false accusations. It was in the night hours when strength and courage are at their lowest ebb that Paul heard Christ's voice speaking to him, "Be of good cheer" (Acts 23:11).

Nowhere in God's Word are we promised exemption from trouble. Neither does He shield us from hard places or sorrow. But He does promise to be with us always. Upon that foundation true cheerfulness can be built. A cheerful heart may not be a gay heart, but it has learned that trust in Christ lifts us up above our circumstances. It puts a song of cheer in our hearts that permeates our whole personality. Cheerfulness is contagious. It can be passed on to others.

Speaking of another, a friend said, "When I met her I was looking down; when I left her I was looking up."

To be habitually hopeful is the best prescription possible for health of body, soul, and spirit. Hope can make the step buoyant, quicken the heart with anticipation, and renew the mind with confidence. Without hope initiative dies.

The psalmist David found himself in a desperate situation. In the natural, things looked hopeless. But David was wise. He refused to let discouragement creep in and paralyze the hope that lived in his heart. Experience had taught him that hope based on faith in God would see him through any time of trouble. In a prayer of confidence and trust David said, "I will hope continually and I will yet praise thee more and more" (Psalm 71:14).

Optimism is all tied up with trust. If I know that I am in His hands, then I know that there is no need to worry or fret. Whatever comes, God will use it for my good. Regardless of circumstances the uplook is always better than the outlook. When a Christian looks back to his past experiences he can see how marvelously God has worked it all out. Then isn't it wisdom to cultivate an optimistic attitude? God's Word confirms this, "And we know that all things work together for good to them that love God . . ." (Romans 8:28).

Every worthwhile thing in this world bears its price tag. High qualities of character are not the result of casual or intermittent desires. (Fluctuating efforts only bring fluctuating returns.) They come through consistent perseverance and determination. Troubling problems, adverse situations, harrassing moments — these are all challenges to prove us. Determination is making up one's mind to do a thing. Persevering is going into partnership with determination.

Paul knew the value of such self-discipline when he said, "But I determined this with myself . . ." (II Corinthians 2:1).

Here was the answer to my questions. These were the character qualities that could fit me for a new assignment in living. And if I strengthened each one in my life my soul would grow tall.

The hour had grown late. In the darkness of my room I sat wrapped in my memories. I thought again of the teacher who had taught me lessons not found in the textbook. I wished that I could hear him say to me, "How are you?"

With head held high and shoulders thrown back I would answer, "Professor, I am cheerful — hopeful — optimistic — persevering — and determined."

*Whatsoever things are true, what-
soever things are just, whatsoever
things are pure, whatsoever things
are lovely, whatsoever things are
of a good report . . . think on these
things.*

— PHILIPPIANS 4:8

Chapter 4

Choosing Memories

"Have you met our new neighbor?" my friend next
door asked me. "She moved in recently and is very
lonely. A few months ago she lost her husband and I
think that she is having a difficult time."

A few days later I called on our new neighbor. She
greeted me at the door with tear-filled eyes and soon
poured out her loneliness. Wrapped tightly in her
memories, clinging desperately to them, she was seeking comfort. But she had found none.

"We were happy together," she told me. "Now everything is changed. All I have left are my memories."

As I left her home I wondered about the rightful
place that memories should hold in one's life. Memories
have the power to either comfort or to torture. Happy
memories may be the forget-me-nots that God gives a
grieving heart to cover the scars of sorrow. Other memories can burn their bitterness deep into the soul.

Is it wise to live in memories? What heart has no
hurting memories? They can be healthy warnings to

31

learn from the experience, or, if magnified, they can become cruel. A very wise friend once counseled me, "Choose carefully the memories that live with you."

There is a very special person on my visiting list. I call her Lady Sunshine. She is a silver-haired lady, who has been an invalid for many years. With a twinkle in her eyes she loves to tell amusing incidents from the past. Her soft laughter makes you share the happiness that she knew. She is alone now but her choice of memories speaks of a heart that rises above its sorrows to share its joys with others.

Memories can be very costly. The memory of an unhappy childhood has embittered many lives. A child, feeling neglected or unloved, may carry the scar for as long as he lives. Memories of hurts, failures, guilt, sorrow can invade the mind and leave in its wake feelings of discouragement and depression.

To dwell upon the memory of an injustice suffered or a wrong endured can do no good, only harm. What a tragedy when one spends so much valuable time remembering the hurts that there is no time to enjoy the good things. What a pity to so narrow one's horizon!

Study courses to improve the memory are very popular today. Many books are written on the subject. A good memory is definitely an asset but one seldom hears about the advantage of being forgetful. Yet it plays a most important part in every Christian's life.

Paul, the apostle, learned the wisdom of putting some things behind him and forgetting them. Remember his words? ". . . Forgetting those things which are behind . . . I press toward the mark . . ." (Philippians 3:13, 14).

Think how comforting it is to us to remember that God has forgiven us of all our sins and remembers them against us no more. They are buried deep in the sea of His forgetfulness.

Forgiveness and forgetfulness must walk hand in hand. To forgive and not forget is not true forgiveness. If personal hurts, offenses, and injuries are harbored in the heart they will do harm. They poison love, tenderness, and friendliness. They taint the spirit with resentment and the heart becomes bitter. Memories such as these hinder the Spirit-filled walk of the Christian. Christ taught us that there is a healing power in the love that can forget self and its rights.

Elizabeth is one of those gracious persons it is a joy to know. Having her for my friend is as lovely as the memory I have of her favorite branch of pale pink apple blossoms in her blue willow bowl. She has a sensitive, artistic nature. Her clever touch made her modest home distinctive and attractive.

As we became friends I learned that Elizabeth was subject to moods of deep depression. Her husband was a kind man, devoted to his family, but he lacked the cultural background of his wife. Their two children were bright, active teen-agers.

Elizabeth's periods of depression became more frequent and longer in duration. I was deeply concerned, wanting to help, yet not knowing how. Then, one day my telephone rang. It was Elizabeth.

"Will you drive with me to a sanitarium outside the city?" she asked. "I have an appointment with the psychiatrist but I do not want to go alone."

It was a beautiful late fall day. The warmth of the autumn sunshine whispered, "Enjoy me today. I will be leaving you soon."

Straggling leaves of red and gold spattered the roadside. We drove along in silence. One felt the beauty of the day with a tinge of sadness. It was like saying "Goodbye" to a departing friend. Then Elizabeth spoke:

"For a long time I have known that I need help. My family has suffered because of my 'bad times.' Yet I have seemed unable to prevent them. I am willing to do anything to overcome the problem."

Perhaps it was this open approach that made it easy for Elizabeth to talk with the doctor. Perhaps it was his kindly manner and his understanding. She talked freely and openly. The intense relief she felt in opening her heart to another showed in her face and voice. At her request the doctor asked me to sit in during their discussion.

Do you know what had caused this lovely woman years of unhappiness? Memories!

"I married against my parents wishes," Elizabeth told the doctor. "We moved a great distance from my family but I have never been able to forget the beautiful home, the social acceptance, and the advantages that I had known. I have wanted them so badly for my family. All of my makeshift attempts to make our home attractive have seemed at times to increase my feelings of frustration and unhappiness. My husband is always kind to us. He is a devoted father. He does for us all that he can. But my memories keep me from what I want most — a heart that knows contentment."

God surely guided Elizabeth in her choice of a doctor. He listened quietly to her story and then he said:

"You want a contented heart? You can have it. But you can find it only in Christ. I recommend for you prayer, God's Word, and a close walk with His Son. When a memory torments you, deliberately replace it with a promise from the Bible or a reassuring thought of His love and care. Look at your blessings through eyes washed with repentant tears. See the priceless treasures that are yours. You have a faithful, loving husband; normal, intelligent children. They ask only for a well mother and a happy home.

"Look at the price tags. Money can buy a house but all the money in the world cannot buy a home. That costs love — understanding — appreciation — giving — sharing — effort.

"It won't be easy, but you can do it. Remember you are a rich woman in the things that really count. New days will turn into new memories. Make them good ones."

Walking across the hospital grounds to the car, Elizabeth stopped and faced me.

"I feel so ashamed," she told me. "To think that I had forgotten the most important thing in the world. I feel so grateful for this reminder."

It isn't often that a story such as Elizabeth's is touched with so much tragedy and sorrow. Neither does the story always have such a victorious ending. Elizabeth learned to turn from the old memories to the reality of her experience with Christ. Day by day she became a more confident and contented woman. She has faced with courage the death of her nineteen-year-old daughter. That was followed with the accidental drownings of her son and his young wife. Recently Elizabeth lost her husband.

I no longer live near Elizabeth but I saw her recently. She told me of her busy days working with small children. No trace of self-pity — no questioning doubts. We talked about the happy memories that we had shared together. When I said goodbye to my friend, I left a wonderful woman whose quiet, restful spirit has made her a blessing to many. Elizabeth, who won the victory over troubling memories.

God never intended us to be prisoners of our memories. Living in the past is the surest way of missing all the opportunities of the present. It keeps you from seeing the new ventures waiting for you — new friends, new experiences, new knowledge, new opportunities for service.

Never does a lonely heart forget the happier days. One would never want that. But there is a truth that should be remembered. It is this. When a lonely woman lives too much in her memories she is blinding and cheating herself.

Learn to not compare the happiness of the past with the new way of life that faces you. Each assignment in living brings its own kind of happiness. Cherish your precious memories but reach out, too, to find the joys at hand.

Each of us is responsible for creating a happy atmosphere wherever she is placed. Friends are quick to give sympathy and help when sorrow comes. But it is selfishness to impose brooding memories on others.

This is no new truth. We find it in God's Word. Paul had fresh memories of loneliness, rejection, persecution, imprisonment. He knew physical weakness and the weariness of pain. In Paul's letter to the Christians in Corinth, he declared that he was determined not to make them sad by dwelling upon his own troubles. And it was Paul who advised us to fix our minds upon things that are lovely, kind, gracious, true.

Minds filled with thoughts such as these will not be troubled by unhappy memories.

Do you see difficulties in every opportunity or opportunities in every difficulty?

— UNKNOWN

Chapter 5

Oh, Yes You Can

Several months passed. It seemed a long time since the night that I accepted in my heart a new assignment in living. Somehow I had expected a new door to open much sooner. Each waiting day brought its own challenge. Morning — noon — night endlessly repeated themselves. Yet there was a tingling feeling of anticipation, a sense of expectation.

Then one day it happened. In the mail came a letter offering me a position in a small church-related college. I had no doubts. I knew that this was the place God had for me. I realized, too, that His timing was right. It had been a difficult lesson to learn to wait for God's time but a most profitable one.

Busy days began. It was not easy to close our home or to put away the keepsakes of many years. There was sadness in the prospect of leaving old and true friends. Thoughts of leaving the familiar places distressed me. Severing ties made strong by long years of association was harder to do than I had thought.

That new life that I had welcomed so gladly seemed frightening in its strangeness. Suddenly all my bright confidence and anticipation deserted me. Panic seized me. Faith, confidence, courage seemed but words that I had used so glibly. Now all at once I did not even know their meaning. It was like close, familiar friends becoming all at once unfriendly strangers.

"I can't do it," I told myself. "I can't go to a strange city — to a strange school — to strange students with all their problems."

I looked about and the emptied rooms filled me with anguish.

"I can't do it," I repeated. "I'll stay here. Surely I can fill my days with usefulness right where I am."

The late afternoon sun gave a last look through the undraped window. I watched it flicker across the floor, touch me gently, then leave the room in the soft grey of twilight. In a strange way I felt quieted.

"Who said that you were going alone?" my heart caught the questions.

"Didn't I promise that I would never leave you; that I would guide you every step of the way?

"Haven't I supplied sufficient strength for every task I have given you?

"Haven't you learned that trust in Me brings peace and heart rest?"

Twilight deepened into darkness. I sat on a low packing box lost in my thoughts. Back, back in the years I went. And out of almost forgotten memories crept a long-ago happening. I smiled, for I remembered it well.

It began with a small dinner party. Summer weather reminded us of vacation time. Our four busy husbands were unable to leave their work but they suggested that we wives take a trip to Colorado.

"Get away from the city heat," they urged us. "Take a trip to the Rockies. Enjoy that wonderful scenery. Visit Pike's Peak — Rampart Range — Garden of the Gods — all the many interesting things there are to see."

Planning was part of the fun of going. All close friends, we studied road maps and read all available brochures. It was late afternoon when we reached our destination. After securing our motel accommodations we decided to take a short ride on one of the scenic roads.

Time slipped by unnoticed and suddenly we realized that it had grown dark. We had been steadily climbing in elevation on a road with sharply winding turns. None of us was an experienced mountain driver for our area was a flat plain.

We saw a sign pointing down to a deep abyss. It read: "The Bottomless Pit."

Fear seized us. Heroically we tried to bolster the jittery nerves of our driver. Anxiously we watched for a place to turn back. Then all at once I read a sign posted high in large, clear letters. It said:

"Oh, *yes* you can; a thousand others have!"

I read it aloud. "Sure we can," one said. Like a chant in singsong voices we repeated the words over and over. And confidence crept back into our car. *Sure* we could!

Safely back in our rooms that night we talked about our experience. We knew that we would never forget those words. As we knelt to pray each woman knew in her heart that the road of life before her might hold many unforeseen turnings. But with His help she could say when the way was frightening, "Others before me have gone this way. Christ brought them through in safety. He will do that for me."

"That was such a long, happy time ago," I thought as I rose from the packing box. But the message was the same. And it brought the encouragement I needed just then. It was fear of a new road that had upset me. I had lost sight of the wonderful new *opportunity* ahead. Now I was ready to begin my new assignment in living. I again felt faith, confidence, and courage — like warm friends standing by to help.

Look about you. Not casually or with indifferent eyes. Look closely with understanding and respect. Hidden by the commonplace you may find a very special person. Someone who has faced a difficult assignment, accepted it, and is turning it into a triumph of faith and courage.

Dolores was a senior in college. An older brother and sister had established high academic records before her. Dolores had come full of fun and laughter, an excited freshman. I came to know her well for she served as part-time typist in my office. One associated a happy face with Dolores. Academically she equaled her brother and sister and her name was high on the dean's honor list.

At the close of her junior year Dolores had married a classmate, a fine fellow. Both were in education and enthusiastic about teaching careers. With high hopes they began their senior year.

It was the week before Thanksgiving. A heavy fog made driving hazardous. Outside the city limits the young husband attempted to pass a car not seeing an oncoming car. A horrible accident resulted. For days Dolores' life hung in the balance. Then we knew. Her life had been spared but gay, happy Dolores was blind.

Second semester was beginning before Dolores was dismissed from the hospital. She was still under doctor's care and a series of plastic surgeries still faced her. Both doctors and nurses marvelled at the courage of the young bride. When her friends were allowed to visit her and fumbled for words to express their sympathy, it was *Dolores* who cheered *them.*

Within a few weeks after her dismissal Dolores began studies in Braille under a blind teacher. He told her, "What you did before your accident you can learn to do now. Nothing can keep you from a rich, full life if you have the courage to face your problem. You can rise above it. Remember that you can do what many, many others have."

Dolores spent three months in a school for the blind. Here she was taught housekeeping, sewing, child care, and safety rules for crossing busy streets. She continued her study in Braille and proved a good student.

When the fall semester began Dolores registered for her senior year. The quick staccato tap of her white cane became a familiar sound as she found her way down long halls to her classrooms. That amazing ability to laugh at her mistakes endeared her to everyone. Together Dolores and her husband planned a future that had no room in it for self-pity.

"What will she do?" concerned friends asked.

Dolores answered that question, "Don't you know? After we finish school I will take special training to teach the blind. My husband will follow his career as a history teacher. God has been so good to us. We are together and together we want to serve Him."

Dark moments must have come to Dolores during those tragic months. Moments of heartbreak. I don't know her moment of acceptance but I do know Dolores. In her heart was a faith that placed herself in God's hands. And Courage whispered to her, "Oh, *yes* you can; thousands of others have!"

"How attractive," I thought when I met the tall, blond wife of a young administrator. Her blue eyes were so friendly and her smile contagious. I chatted with her and enjoyed her quick wit and laughter. A little later I watched from across the room as her husband bent over and gently helped her to her feet.

"Isn't it sad?" a friend standing near me murmured. "She's so young to face such a dreary future. You know that they have three young children. Rheumatoid arthritis is such a crippling disease."

Three years have passed and I have watched this lovely family. They are busy with family projects, happy and active. Never have I heard Rita utter one word of complaint. There are days when the telephone must go unanswered when the pain is too severe for her to be up. But there are other days. Days when she plans surprises for her family or when she reaches out to encourage a friend or to share a problem. Every day her family finds expressions of her love. Laughter lives easily in this home. Thoughtfulness and helpfulness dwell there, too.

One day Rita and I talked together. Her hands are quite misshapen now and pain is a familiar companion. At times walking is difficult and the shadow of a wheelchair moves closer.

"Can you tell me," I asked her, "how you have accepted this affliction so courageously?"

Rita smiled and answered, "I had no choice to accept or to reject this crippling disease. But I did have a choice in my attitude toward it. First, there is my family. My illness is sure to affect them but I can brighten it for them by not allowing it to make me discouraged and unhappy. I am determined that my children will know a normal, happy family life. A wearisome mother makes a wearisome home.

"Each day I find my source of strength through my relationship with Christ. When I am tempted to feel sorry for myself I have only to look about me. I can see others carrying heavy burdens uncomplainingly."

Her eyes smiled as she finished, "It is a continual battle. Yesterday's victory will not do for today. But with His help I can say, 'You can do it today. Oh, *yes* you can!'"

Late one afternoon I shopped in a Woolworth store. My time was limited and I waited impatiently at the cash register for my change and purchase. I looked to see what was delaying my saleslady. Then I really saw her. She was middle-aged and she looked dreadfully tired. She was trying to complete my sale but looked so upset that I asked her if she were ill. Quick tears came to her eyes.

"I am sorry to be so slow," she apologized. "This is my first day to work here and my mind seems to be all confused. I have to work but maybe I am too old to learn."

"Of course you are not too old," I assured her. "Anyone is naturally nervous and unsure of herself while learning new procedures. But you can do it. Look at the other employees. They went through the training period, too.

"I'll tell you a secret. I am learning a new job, too. Sometimes it seems too big for me. Then I turn to prayer and I find help. Each day as I face my duties

I remind myself — 'Oh, *yes* you can. A million others have!' "

I took away the memory of her shy smile and her promise to try it for herself. No life is exempt from difficult problems. The small boy struggling to learn his multiplication tables — the young girl who can't stand math — the college student carrying a heavy load and working long hours to pay his expenses — the father carrying the pressure of finances — the mother with her endless tasks. These are normal anxieties.

But what of the times when one is forced to face problems that go deep into the very soul? Overwhelming problems, painful, with no visible answers? These are times when the heart can find help only in Christ.

No, no one is exempt. But always remember that He waits to give us the courage to say, "Oh, yes, I can find courage with His help. Countless others have. I can do it, too."

Politeness is a small price to pay for the goodwill and affections of others.

— UNKNOWN

Chapter 6

Lonely?

Loneliness is universal. It is common to all. Loneliness can strike when one is surrounded by friends or can dog the footsteps of a stranger in a strange place. It brings nostalgia for the past and creates fear for the future.

Loneliness is many things. It hides behind sorrow; cringes when it feels ignored; yields to moods of despondency; fancies itself unloved and unappreciated; longs for the familiar; cries because it feels alone.

Years ago, when I was a freshman, a beloved teacher told me something that I have never forgotten. Mary Scott was a tall, angular woman in her early fifties. In spite of her austere manner she was a popular figure on the campus. In repose her face was stern and her black eyes piercing. One quaked in her class if the lesson was unprepared — but very soon we learned to watch for her smile. It would begin in her eyes then slowly the sharp lines would crumple into warmth and gentleness.

As my school years passed my admiration for this rare teacher grew. She encouraged me to explore the world of good books. She helped me to discover for myself new interests of study. It was she who noticed my intense interest in the manners and customs of the Bible lands and guided me in that field of specialization.

Mary Scott was quite alone in the world, entirely without family ties. But, somehow, you never thought of her as being alone or ever lonely. One day I talked with her about the loneliness I felt at times. She said, "Let me tell you something I learned a long time ago. I was alone in a large city, very alone and miserably lonesome. I spent hours in the public library reading and brooding. Opening a small book one afternoon I read these words.

> Every heart knows loneliness. One may live in a house of luxury, or in a modest home with only limited comforts. One may live in shabbiness with only the bare necessities. It makes no difference. Every heart at times feels the ache of loneliness.

"I have forgotten the rest that I read but those words have remained with me. If loneliness is shared by everyone, I decided, then I can accept those times with understanding and plain common sense. Instead of dwelling on my lonely feelings I will deliberately set out to show cheerful friendliness to everyone I meet. Throughout the years I have practiced this. It has helped me to push loneliness into the background and to emphasize the pleasant things that each day brings."

My teacher could grade me only "E" for effort, I am afraid. Too often I have been slow in rising above the lonely times. But her example has prodded me on to persistent effort. I have discovered that it helps, it really does. I have learned, too, that the most cheerful persons are not those least invaded by loneliness. They are the conquerors!

Look about you. Look carefully. You will find courageous women who face a specialized type of loneliness every day of their lives. It is a loneliness that another cannot share.

Remember that little Alabama girl born in 1880? That beloved first baby adored by her family? When only nineteen months old Helen Keller became suddenly blind and deaf. No memories to cherish of the blue sky; the song of a little bird; the fragile loveliness of a flower. How could she know why the soft patter of rain touched her face? Her parent's faces were unknown.

The story of Helen and her teacher, Miss Anne Sullivan, is well known. She came into the little girl's life when Helen was five and a whole new world opened to her. Out of the dark silence Helen Keller found real meaning for her life. She found comfort for her own deep loneliness in helping others who lived in blindness and heard no sounds. She found a spiritual faith that satisfied her heart needs and she turned to the world a smiling face. Helen Keller's story has encouraged countless others to defy handicaps and find rich and full lives.

Examples of such splendid courage are all about us. Such a one was Rhea. She came to college a shy, insecure freshman. When speaking to you her troubled eyes never left your face and you felt her uncertainty. Her smile and manner were always pleasantly courteous but she was a lonely little figure.

Soon Rhea's secret was discovered. Rhea was becoming deaf. Her high school years had been difficult. Doctors told her that very soon she would lose all hearing. Determined to have an education, Rhea came to college. Lip reading made the lectures understandable but when an instructor's face was not clearly visible her notes became sketchy and her grades suffered.

A kindly dean explained to Rhea the advantages of attending a college for the deaf. It hurt to watch her struggle for acceptance of her problem. Contacts were made and Rhea went for an interview. She spent several days at this school and came back smiling.

"I saw so many others who cannot hear," she told me. "But they are happy and training for worthwhile careers. I can do that, too. And I won't be so lonely. I have accepted my handicap now and I will find happiness."

Have you ever thought of "occupational loneliness"? A former member of this surprisingly large group talked with me recently. Joanne is now a high school teacher. She began her teaching career at the age of thirty-nine. After years of successful work in the business world she had become weary in mind and body and turned to the educational area.

"How would you define loneliness?" I asked Joanne.

"Define it?" she grinned. "It was my chief occupation for many years. I worked at being lonely. Really, I made quite a success of it, too."

Joanne's childhood had been clouded by the divorce of her parents. A very sensitive child, she was torn between love for her father and her mother. Even as a young girl she realized that her mother was emotionally ill. Joanne had barely reached her teens when her mother had to be taken away for treatment. Lone-

48

liness by then had become Joanne's constant companion. As time passed she knew that her mother would never be well enough to come home again.

Painfully aware that her home background was different from most of her classmates,' Joanne brooded over her unhappiness. She was a bright student and after high school she put herself through college. Joanne became a reserved young woman, fiercely independent. She tried to conceal the loneliness that was like a gnawing pain destroying contentment and peace of mind. But it showed in her face and her words.

When a position opened in a city far from her native state Joanne accepted it. She made new friends and the years passed pleasantly — except for this deep loneliness that followed wherever she went. Gradually Joanne realized that if she were ever to know real heart rest the brooding loneliness must be conquered. But how? Perhaps facing it was the beginning. Her increasing interest in teaching persuaded her to resign her position. She went back to college to pick up some needed education courses and it was here that I met Joanne.

As her first year of teaching came to a close, I noticed the change in Joanne. Not over night did it happen but gradually, step by step. I could see it in her absorbing interest in her lively sophomore classes. In the quick flashes of humor that sparkled her words. In her complete enjoyment of her new apartment. All these, but most of all in her own words.

"Yes," Joanne told me, "loneliness was my chief occupation. It absorbed my thoughts. It closed my day and greeted me each morning. I am still alone but I am finding that that is a very foolish reason for not being happy. I have begun to put into practice a practical application of Christ's words. He gave us a command — 'Be of good cheer.' He *expects* it of me."

Occupational loneliness? It exists. Guard against it. Never coddle loneliness. If you do, it will act as a spoiled child demanding more attention and pampering. Christ spoke often of joy and good cheer. Never did He put the emphasis upon happiness. That is a fleeting thing — something happens and the heart glows with happiness — but a telephone call, a letter, a spoken word, and happiness as quickly disappears, leaving the ache of unhappiness. Nothing, however, can destroy the joy that comes through fellowship with Christ and the cheerful spirit it nurtures.

A loneliness that is understood and faced is like a clean wound that will heal naturally. But there are those who suffer from loneliness yet never understand its cause. This is the do-it-to-yourself kind of loneliness.

Today's market is filled with do-it-yourself kits of all kinds. By following instructions one can paint a lovely picture or turn a plain piece of furniture into a thing of beauty. Do it yourself, but always carefully follow the directions. How sad that a human heart can be lonely for pleasant contacts with others yet fail to follow the rules that make it possible.

Myrtle Reiben lived alone in a modern apartment in a southern city. She had grown up in this city, married, and raised two daughters there. She fluttered about seeking news like a bee seeking honey. Her apartment neighbors learned to expect the quiet opening of her door whenever the outside door opened. Telephone calls from her interrupted their very early morning sleep. She intruded upon afternoon guests or evening enjoyments. Mrs. Reiben's enjoyment in going places was matched only by her ingenious ways of obtaining transportation. Her desire to impress and her craving for prestige were pathetic. And always she blamed others for avoiding her.

Some very fine qualities were found in Myrtle Reiben. She was friendly and eager for callers. She took pride in keeping her nicely furnished apartment in perfect order. Any responsibility given her by any organization in which she was interested was faithfully fulfilled.

But Myrtle Reiben was a lonely person. Any indifference shown her was interpreted as a slight without cause. Any refusal to grant a request was rudeness on the part of the other. Firmly fixed in her mind was an image of herself as a gracious lady admired for her kind, sweet ways.

What a pity that Myrtle Reiben never really looked within herself for the answer to her loneliness — for the answer lay there.

Sometimes we smile as we speak of husbands whose work keeps them away from home much of the time, We tease their wives about being "work widows." I have watched with friendly interest two women face this special kind of loneliness.

One couple moved to our city from a distant eastern state. His new position meant almost continuous travel. It was a most difficult time for his wife. She never quite accepted it. She found no interests to fill her days. Gradually her health began to fail and her doctor told her that her nerves were causing much of her trouble. She is waiting for the day that her husband will retire so they can move "back home."

The second couple came from a northern city. Weekends are the only time this husband can be home. They have no children. His wife is a shy but charming woman who finds the weekends the bright spot in her life. But she did not brood over her loneliness. She has studied music, and long hours of practice on the organ have brought her much pleasure. Now she has added a study of the Spanish language. Realizing that her shyness was keeping her from making friends, she began to accept invitations and to give them. She has made her days pleasantly full.

It is true that two different personalities react differently to the same conditions. One woman may have more endurance and self-reliance than the other. One may be more aggressive, the other may find that staying home is the easiest way to escape meeting strangers.

It is also true that a healthy interest in others and a participation in some interesting activities can make a lonely situation much more pleasant. Surely it is worth trying.

Perhaps it is the lonely, older woman who suffers most. There is the empty stillness of a home that comes when the last child has stepped out alone to meet life. That is *mother-loneliness*. A still deeper loneliness settles over the older woman when her life's companion is taken. Desperately she clings to the old ways, old habits, old associations. Change is difficult and dependence isn't sweet.

> Grow old along with me,
> The best is yet to be.

Down the years hearts have responded to Browning's words. Lovers have caught the glimpse of companionship with a beloved one through all the sunset years.

But there are no poetic lines that tell of joy in walking the last way *alone*. Only the pen of divinely inspired writers gives that assurance. God's Word tells of joy in unbroken fellowship with Christ. It speaks of joy in the changelessness of His Word. It tells of the joy that is prepared for us in heaven.

Everyone needs friends, and the lonely, older woman most of all. There is an art in being a good friend. Long-time friendships do not just happen — they are carefully tended.

What is friendship?

Friendship is living on a two way street. It is giving as well as receiving. Friendship is respecting the "no trespassing" sign that permits a friend his right to privacy and to his own opinions. It is confidence in the other's motives while not expecting perfection in his actions. It is being quick to praise and slow to criticize. Friendship is sharing experiences without depending overmuch on the other. It is enjoying a friend without monopolizing. It is diligently keeping the simple rules of lasting friendships.

Since friendships are so important to the lonely woman, wouldn't it be wise to stop now and then to take inventory? What characteristics do my friends see in me? Any irritating habits?

Answer these questions honestly and nudge yourself if any betrays you.

Do I have the monologue habit? Too talkative?

Am I inclined to be set in my opinions? Do I become argumentative?

Am I guilty of discussing family affairs with outsiders?

Am I quick to offer unsolicited advice?

Do I talk too much about my physical ailments?

Am I an inquisitive neighbor who pries into another's business?

Am I a gossiper?

Do I feel possessive toward a friend and resent the rights of other friends?

A few years ago a prayer for the older person was published in a city newspaper. It expresses some very common needs. I liked its humor. The ability to smile at one's frailties is a healthy indication that the petitioner is a well-balanced, in-the-middle-of-the-road kind of a person.

Prayer for Older Folks

Lord, thou knowest that I am growing older.

Keep me from becoming too talkative, and particularly keep me from falling into the tiresome habit of expressing an opinion on every subject.

Release me from the craving to straighten out everybody's affairs.

Keep my mind free from the recital of endless details. Give me wings to get to the point.

Give me the grace, dear Lord, to listen to the others describe their aches and pains. Help me to endure the boredom with patience and to keep my lips sealed. For my own aches and pains are increasing in number and intensity and the pleasure of discussing them is becoming sweeter as the years go by.

Teach me the glorious lesson that, occasionally, I might be mistaken.

Keep me reasonably sweet; I do not wish to be a saint (saints are so hard to live with) but a sour old woman is the crowning work of the devil.

Make me thoughtful, but not moody; helpful, but not pushy; independent, yet able to accept with graciousness favors that others wish to bestow upon me.

Free me of the notion that simply because I have lived a long time I am wiser than those who have not lived so long.

If I do not approve of some of the changes that have taken place in recent years, give me the wisdom to keep my mouth shut.

Lord, You know that when the end comes I would like to have a friend or two left.

Amen!

— Author Unknown

Food for thought, isn't it?

God makes the rims in which we are placed, but we ourselves can make our lives what we will within the rims.

— Mrs. A. D. Whitney

Chapter 7

Respect Closed Doors

There is something intriguing about a closed door. What does it shut out? What does it shut in? Who may legitimately open it? Who is barred? A door is important. It can say, "Come in, you are welcome." Or it can say, "Please don't intrude."

Holiday doors are such *happy* doors. A holly wreath with its festive red bow can magically turn a door into a warm, friendly invitation to share with all the world the goodwill of the Christmas season.

Some doors seem to reflect the personalities of their owners. They invite friendly callers — good times — quiet talks — all that the word *sharing* means.

Once I walked through the streets of Jerusalem. Small, flat-roofed houses, looking like boxes, perched precariously on the hillsides. Shutters closed the windows from curious eyes. Plain, heavy doors shut the family in safely and seemed to say to outsiders, "Stay out!" Inside, I knew, lived happy families with welcome guests. But I was a stranger, and to me the doors seemed forbidding and unfriendly.

On a maple-lined street of a town in the valley of the Susquehana River stands an old house, sedate among its elderly neighbors. I grew up in that rambling house and love every niche and corner.

Strangers own it now and when a few years ago I visited my hometown I walked past the old homeplace. I felt the windows of my old room blinking at me reproachfully — they had known me through all my girlhood years. "Aren't you coming in?" they seemed to ask. The wide front porch invited me to rest and visit awhile. I was tempted — oh, *how* I was tempted! But I looked at the door. It was closed. It seemed to frown a bit and remind me: "I'm sorry, but you don't live here any more. Others have taken your place and you must not intrude."

"You're right," I admitted and walked slowly away with a backward glance of farewell.

Yes, doors are important. And closed doors may have a special meaning.

Perhaps to no one else does a closed door have the same significance that it does to the lonely woman. Loneliness has a way of making one super-sensitive and quick to imagine intended slights. Many times she feels left out. One of the hardest things she has to do is to accept the door that is closed by the marriage of a son or daughter.

Mother-in-law jokes, heard so often, make me cringe. It is such a cruel way to score a laugh at the expense of hurting another. So rarely is it balanced by a merited tribute.

No two mothers are alike. Motherhood is no magic wand that, waved over a new mother, produces all the ideal qualifications. Mothers are persons. Each has her individual personality, background, tastes, desires, hopes. Each has her strengths and weaknesses. But by far the majority of mothers love their children and want only the best for them.

When the "alone years" come, it is a wise mother who looks back and remembers. Remembers back to when she was a young woman raising her family. A young wife feels very possessive of her husband. She does not see in him the traces of the boy that his mother treasures. She sees the man who is her husband and who belongs to her and their children. It is sad when there is rivalry between a man's wife and mother. And, because she has traveled the path and knows the way, it is the wisest of mothers who gently closes the door — from the *outside*. Doors that are closed in love and understanding are never hostile doors. They open often with affection to share family times together.

Many a widowed mother would be shocked and deeply hurt if it were suggested that her desire to keep a son or daughter close was selfishness on her part. Such a one was Bob's mother.

It was May. Bob and Elaine were graduating from college. They had been engaged to be married for some months and had looked forward to a June wedding. Elaine had a contract to teach in the city where Bob had a position waiting for him. Then, suddenly, Bob's father died. Bob had been raised on a farm, the only son with two older sisters. His father had been deeply disappointed when he chose a business career rather than farming.

Now the young couple was troubled. Bob's mother was wrapped in her grief and this made their plans seem selfish. She was unwilling to leave her old home, though financially well able to live comfortably in the small town nearby. Her married daughters lived very near her.

The closer graduation approached the more depressed Bob's mother became. And the more troubled Bob and Elaine became. Together the young couple went to a marriage counselor.

"Should I give up my chosen profession and go back to the farm?" Bob asked him.

After several interviews Bob made his decision. He went to his mother and spoke as a son matured and responsible.

"We love you, Mother," he told her, "And you will always be cared for. But Elaine and I must live our own lives as we feel best. We are accepting the positions offered us and we will be looking forward to your first visit in our new home."

Faced with this decision Bob's mother found a small house in town. Weekly visits from her daughters and frequent weekend trips by Bob and Elaine assured her family that she was making friends and finding new interests. True, she was lonely at times for the farm and the old days. But family ties were secure and her new independence brought its own inner reward. By closing the door Bob and Elaine had forced his mother to grow and had reserved for themselves their rightful place in her life.

A few months ago I visited my son and my daughter-in-law. It is such fun to leave the plane and find two excited little-boy faces watching for me at the gate. And behind them the lovely face of my daughter-in-law. I wish that you could meet her for she is one of my dearest friends.

One late afternoon I sat by the large window with my baby granddaughter. I watched as the colors of evening caressed the mountaintops. Softly they covered them with a blanket of deepest purple. Then, like a whispered "Good night" the last trace of rose and gold slipped from sight. I love that mountain view. Its changing colors are as variable as the many moods of a human heart and they charm me always.

The door opened and my son was home from his day at the hospital. With a quick smile for his tiny daughter and a light, "Did you have a pleasant day, Mom?" he hurried to the kitchen. I could hear his voice as he told his wife the happenings of the day. A new patient, a problem — husband-and-wife talk.

I looked at the sleeping mountains and remembered the noisy bang of the door that always announced my son was home from school. Hungry, then ready for play, he would stop to tell me about his day at school.

Below me I saw the twinkling lights of the city. I remembered the hurrying years — high school, college, the medical student. I thought again of the quiet talks, the confiding times.

Our baby's nodding little head nestled down on my shoulder. I heard again the voices in the kitchen. A husband talking to his wife. I smiled at the sleepy baby and I thought, "How right it is — how very right. This is a closed door that tells a mother that all is right with her family."

There is a door that opens to couples that the woman alone is not always free to enter. No one should feel slighted; wistful maybe, but not critical. With a twinge of hurt the widowed woman may think back to happier days when "they" were part of the group.

Usually guests at dinner parties are an even number. Being the "odd" guest isn't always a happy arrangement. There are exceptions, of course. I know an older woman who is often included in a much younger group simply because she is such stimulating company. Nevertheless, there are times when the single woman must face the fact that she is not included in a married group. Allowing depression to take over will not change the matter. That would only bring on an acute attack of self-pity. Accepting the situation graciously, with understanding, keeps the incident in its proper dimensions — not too big — not too important.

There is a door that should read, "Mothers — Keep Out!"

Too harsh? Unkind? Unfair? Please lay aside your personal feelings and think seriously about it.

Berta Nisson and her husband adopted a three-day-old baby girl. Little Cathy was loved deeply — "smothered with love."

In her early teens Cathy was treated for an emotional problem. Her concerned parents never understood that their possessive love for their adopted daughter was the cause of Cathy's problem.

At twenty Cathy married a boy she had known since childhood. The young couple wanted to move into an apartment of their own but her mother pleaded with tears, "We own this duplex. You will have your own home and yet you will be under one roof with us." Then followed the tearful reminder that swayed Cathy every time she expressed a desire of her own, "Have you forgotten that we took you when you were only three days old? Your natural mother deserted you. We have given you every advantage possible for us to give. Now we are growing old and you want to leave us."

Cathy and Ed lived in the duplex rent free. ("To help you get started," her mother said.) More meals were eaten with "the folks" than cooked by the young bride. Furnishings met with mother's approval. When baby Steven was born it was grandmother who took over the care of the new baby. And grandfather took over the place that a new father dreams of for himself in the life of his little son.

It was inevitable that trouble would come. Ed became restless then openly resentful. Cathy was torn between her parents and her husband. Soon after Baby Shirley was born Cathy faced heartbreak. Rarely did Ed spend an evening at home. When he did he was silent and withdrawn. Cathy felt ill with fear.

One night Ed did not return. Cathy received a letter in which he asked for his freedom.

"We have never had a home," he wrote, "only an extension of your parents'. I have found other interests and I want to be free."

Cathy talked with me about her problem. Beneath her quiet manner I found emotions seething with frustrations and bitterness.

"My life has been lived for me," she confided. "I have wished many times that I hadn't been the child chosen. I have wondered if my debt to them will *ever* be paid. I haven't rebelled for myself but my children *must* be allowed to think for themselves and to make their own decisions."

Cathy's story is not as unusual as one might think. It is unfortunate when parents, and more often mothers, fail to untie the apron strings. It is never easy to stand back and watch one's children learn lessons by trial and error. It isn't easy to keep from offering free advice. It isn't easy to refrain from suggesting better child training methods. It isn't easy to remember that this is a closed door. No, it isn't easy — but it pays rich dividends.

The closed door. Much depends upon who closes it.

There is one door that opens to a host of problems, more, perhaps, than any other: "Should a widowed mother live with a married son or daughter?" Immediately we acknowledge the fact that there are exceptions to every rule. Each case is individual in its circumstances; unique in its needs.

In grandmother's day it was expected that the children would take their widowed mother and care for her. If there were several children, usually the time was divided and Mother rotated from one child's home to another. It was that way in my mother's family. I had one of the dearest of grandmothers and well remember how happy I was when it was our turn to have Grandmother with us.

Today most grandmothers live far more active lives with independent interests. Modern medical care is available. Television and radio keep her informed and entertained. Church activities offer involvement.

But yesterday or today there is the problem of loneliness and old age. When the door opens with the invitation, "You may live with us," the heart impulsively answers, "I will. I don't want to be alone." But the mind hesitates and then suggests, "Think it over carefully. Consider all the angles." Wise to do that, don't you think?

It has been interesting to watch the results of some of these decisions.

Ruth Coleman was the wife of a successful professional man. A capable person, she was extremely happy in her role. With definite and decided views she brought up her only daughter, who was in many ways much like her mother. She also enjoyed organizations and loved to "run things."

In her older, widowed years Ruth Coleman was a mixture of fine, likable traits and a caustic, critical attitude — generous with those she loved, harsh with any one who crossed her. Any enjoyment from her company was dimmed by her incessant talking and unquenchable suggestions. Her sentences always began with, "Now I think," with emphasis on the *I*.

She was unhappy living alone so she sold her home and went to live with her married daughter. With three grandchildren in the home it was necessary for Ruth Coleman to take the guest room. Soon the entire house was run under her supervision.

A wrong decision? Perhaps. Ruth Coleman would be the last person to believe that her family had sacrificed privacy, family discussions, fun times, personal views, and rightful responsibilities. Neither will she ever realize that there are times when her hand should quietly close the door and allow her daughter's family to be alone.

Elsie Darrow was a widow when I met her. First impressions of her were a bit vague — drab in dress, drab in personality. Her manner was almost servile but beneath the surface Elsie Darrow was a woman of rigid opinions and a strong will.

Her older years were the saddest that I know. A long, deep-seated fear of being alone had become a phobia. An unfriendly relationship with her only daughter-in-law and complete disapproval of her own daughter's way of living made it impossible to live with either.

What happened? Elsie Darrow became a transient guest. She stayed with a friend or relative until circumstances ended the visit, then on to another friend's home — willing to do almost anything to avoid living alone.

What a dreary road to walk through one's last years! Elsie Darrow's case may be an extreme one but it teaches a lesson. A self-reliant contentment does not come suddenly. It is the reward of accumulating through the years that inner strength that can make even living alone a challenging adventure.

Yet, every rule has its exceptions: There was "Aunt Emma" to Peggy and all of her friends. She was a frail little lady with a twinkle in her eye and a quick, perky manner. When Peggy had been left an orphan at twelve years of age Aunt Emma became her foster mother. They lived in a very small town where Aunt Emma was the only telephone operator. The switchboard was installed in her home. She had never married but children loved her and Peggy grew up secure and happy.

After high school Aunt Emma watched with pride as Peggy studied to become a nurse. The night that Peggy graduated Aunt Emma was the happiest woman in the auditorium. *Later Peggy married and Aunt Emma beamed with delight when she spoke of Peggy's little girls.

A heart condition forced Aunt Emma to give up her work but there was no question about her future — Peggy's husband came for her and took her "home." Never did any one feel that Peggy's care of Aunt Emma was in payment for the care she had received. It was given because Aunt Emma was just Aunt Emma — a very special person.

While this proves that there are no set rules, yet there is no contradiction. In the sharing of another's home there must be a delicate balance between family participation and personal reserve and respect for the privacy of each. A congenial relationship depends upon it.

Yes, doors *are* important — closed doors — open doors.

*Happiness is everywhere, and its
spring is in our own hearts.*

— JOHN RUSKIN

Chapter 8

That Assignment Called Retirement

Birthdays have the disturbing habit of flying by with incredible swiftness. That is, the birthdays that belong to the older woman. And to the business or professional woman there is one marked, "Special." Plans may have been made long in advance for this particular event. At times this future and safely remote occasion has all the alluring attractiveness of a pleasant daydream. But as the time grows closer and closer the daydream-colors disappear and it becomes stark reality. A reality that, whether or no, must be accepted. This is the birthday that presents retirement.

It would be helpful if a little book of instructions came with the new experience. Yet no list could fit all the needs. Hearts have a way of not always conforming to rules. Each life is uniquely different from all others. And each woman must meet her retirement and shape it to meet her individual needs.

To the one facing retirement health and financial problems may be important factors. But the greatest problem lies within the heart and mind of each woman. It asks the question, "How can retirement bring to me experiences that will give meaning to my life and be satisfying?"

Retirement policies, social security, savings — all these ease the strain of reduced income. But there are other needs — personal, *demanding* needs. And this enforced inactivity offers a dangerous threat to them. To some it may come as an unwelcome intrusion in a well-established pattern of living. Its unfamiliar strangeness often creates feelings of apprehension. For many it is an unwanted, unwelcome change.

Time has a way of blurring memories. The disappointments, the heartaches, the feelings of dissatisfaction, of failures, of loneliness — these tend to fade when the established order is threatened. Looking back, the old ways take on the security of the familiar and the heart reaches out to hold it fast.

Really, what is retirement? A new assignment in living! Time refuses to stand still. Nothing can remain forever unchanged. When retirement is accepted graciously the postworking days can be lived triumphantly. They can become a song of victory for lessons learned, for work achieved. They can be a song of faith accepting the challenge of new experiences.

To the child of God the retirement years have a meaning not known to the one who walks the way alone. That heart has had preparation. It has learned to trust and to "fear not." Life for the Christian is a well-charted course. Safe in the center of God's will nothing can touch that life without His knowledge. And out of His abundant love come comfort and help.

Last years can be blessed years. Best of all, the end of the walk leads directly into the presence of the Lord of lords and King of kings. To be with Christ throughout all eternity is the crowning blessing of the Christian's life.

One would be considered foolish to start on a long journey without packing a suitcase carrying personal needs. But no more foolish than to face retirement without thought or preparation. Personalities differ but there are some basic qualities needed.

Make sure that you take with you a double supply of a sense of humor. You will need it; every day you will need it. And on the days that you feel most alone you will need it most of all. Learn to laugh with yourself.

It was a dismal, rainy day. I felt the warnings of an on-coming attack of the blues. Standing at my window I watched two husky robins fighting over one lonely worm.

With an ear cocked to the ground the first robin listened, then began vigorously to dig in the soft dirt. His companion watched and immediately decided that this was the exact spot for him and began to dig, too. I was fascinated as I watched the tussle. Furiously the first robin pulled and pulled. Just as determined, his opponent pulled and pulled. Then it happened. Both birds had the same worm and it turned into a tug-of-war. With one last pull the poor worm was torn in half and each greedy robin claimed its share of the victory.

There was nothing remarkable in the amusing incident. Just two ridiculous robins fighting over their dinner. But I laughed aloud. It was still raining but the day picked up its lagging spirits and I turned cheerfully to the routine tasks.

All about us are touches of humor. Like happy elves

they wait to turn up the corners of the mouth — if one only stops to notice. Practice looking for them. They can add such bright color to the day.

Peggy and Eleanor were sisters. Raised in the same home their backgrounds and educational advantages were the same. Yet there was a marked difference in the attitudes of the two. Retirement years only emphasized it.

Eleanor was a complainer. What she had was never quite what she wanted. What she wanted was always just out of reach. However blue her skies she invariably found a cloudy spot. Left alone early in her married life she lived a narrow, self-centered life. Her complaining spirit colored her voice and manner. Her cheerlessness was depressing.

Peggy had been a happy, laughing girl. Things tangled up for her sometimes but nothing was ever wrong for very long. She had a way of trusting and smiling. When retirement years came, the word *alone* did not frighten her. Her world was filled with friends, books, and many, many interests.

One sister sighed — the other smiled. One bemoaned her fate — the other counted her blessings. One chose to mope — the other to hope. The difference lay in the attitudes of the two sisters. A faith and trust that tingled with hope and expectation brought to Peggy complete involvement in living each day to the fullest. A dissatisfied, complaining heart had shrunk Eleanor's small world until life had become but a bleak existence.

Have you provided for yourself a genuine interest in others? You will need it for happy retirement. Life is never a solo performance. We are very dependent upon others. Without friendly contacts a life is lonely. The postman's greeting, the paper boy, the pleasant checker at the supermarket, the smile of a passerby — these are friendly touches that brighten a day.

Sometimes in the enjoyment of old friends it is easy to neglect the making of new ones. Familiar faces have such a comfortable appeal. But wake up to your need. Friends who have shared the years with you are priceless. Cherish them gently. But reach out to the added stimulation of fresh contacts. New friends can add sparkle to old ways of thinking and doing.

There is a fragile gift that will add immeasurable loveliness to your life. It is within the reach of all, yet there are some who hurry by with never a glance at this delicate treasure. It is called the gift of appreciation.

A true woman responds to beauty as naturally as a flower to the sun. God splashed this world of ours with colors so vibrant and strong that they stir the very depths of the soul. And the delicate handiwork and pastel loveliness of His creation make the heart throb with the tenderness of its beauty. It is all there — but one must *look* to see.

It was an early winter day years ago. The cold, stinging mist increased my homesickness. We had moved to this midwest city too recently to have made friends and I was keenly missing the old ties.

Shivering, I held fast to the small hand of my three-year-old son as we left the doctor's office. My head was throbbing and my body ached. Anxious only to hurry home I pulled his short steps up to match my hurrying ones, only half hearing his insistent, "Muver, stop!"

Waiting to cross the busy street I looked down into a tearful, upturned face.

"I asked you, Muver, to stop. I want to go back."

Tugging at my hand he drew me back to the windows of a large florist shop. Its beauty was breathtaking. Flowers of softest pink to deepest rose offered their loveliness to the rainy greyness outside.

With his small face pressed close to the window he murmured, "Its so beautiful it hurts me here," and he touched his heart.

I bent and held him close as I told him, "Darling, thank you for showing me this beauty. Thank you for sharing it with me."

I had no money to enter this exclusive shop and buy its flowers. But all this beauty was mine for the taking. Just a few golden moments and it was mine to remember always. As we turned toward home I knew that I was a better, wiser woman.

"Help me, Lord," I whispered in my heart. "Help me to look for beauty in the everydayness of my life. To trace the loveliness of Your handiwork even in the dark and trying days. Help me to carefully guard this gift of appreciation in the heart of my little son."

Close your eyes and remember. What lovely pictures do you recall? What moments of exquisite beauty? When did it happen? Many years ago? Yesterday? Open your eyes now. There are new moments of loveliness to discover.

Marie Rutherford is a young woman whose apartment window looks out upon a neighbor's unattractive back yard. A decrepit garage and tired, sagging clotheslines huddle together beneath a large tree. Those neighbors would be amazed if they knew that they were giving to this woman moments of sheer enjoyment.

Living on the second floor, her favorite chair faces a large window. And like magic it becomes a frame for a picture of living beauty.

"I have four originals," Marie Rutherford smiled. "I have four originals that money cannot buy.

"In the springtime the green lace of the treetop branches sways in the breeze like dressed up little girls learning to curtsy.

"Spring is for hope. After the long, cold winter it is the promise of warmth and sunshine.

"Then summer comes and the picture changes. Deep green leaves soften the glare of the hot sun. Summer concerts are given daily, with rehearsals at sun-rise by the small songsters who set up housekeeping in the widespread branches.

"Summer is the fulfillment of the promise of spring. Even the green of a shade tree reflects the careful handiwork of its Creator.

"Autumn, and the picture is a blaze of golden glory. Yellow leaves calling for attention — yellow leaves drenched with rain — yellow leaves waving a goodbye to summer as they flutter to the ground.

"There is a twinge of sadness in this picture. Summer seemed so short and the long winter months so close at hand. But it has a courage of its own. It speaks of harvest time and the joy of fulfillment. Not even the thought of barren winter branches can curb the exuberant saluting of its colors.

"The winter scene is the most loved of all. Shorn of every covering of beauty, the treetop stands in simple dignity revealing its strength and endurance. Winter snows may bend its boughs but it stands secure in the girded strength of the mother trunk. Up and down the branches scamper squirrels, their bushy tails bobbing a cheerful 'Hi' to the world.

"The loveliest moment comes at sunset. Through the

barren branches the rose and gold of the setting sun shine like an evening benediction. Who cares if the neighbor's yard is dreary and drab? Who wants to look down when all this loveliness is mine if I just look up?"

Too often we fail to appreciate beauty because it wears such a familiar old dress. Have you ever counted the small courtesies shown you in just one day? Try it. That fellow shopper who opened the door for you — the young boy who picked up the package you dropped and gave you a wide, teen-age grin — the neighbor who brought a piece of freshly baked cake, and the flower from a friend's garden — that stranger who in passing smiled and said, "Good morning" — the friendly telephone call — and that cheery letter. These are little things, but the gift of appreciation sees them as special blessings.

Better make sure that you are well supplied with a generous amount of plain common sense. You will need it in large, daily doses. It will help you to recognize boundary lines and keep you from being unhappy about them.

There are boundary lines of health, work, and activities that must be respected. If one must be restricted in any of these, isn't it foolish to rebel and make yourself and others miserable?

One woman I know has been a wheelchair invalid for eighteen years. She absorbed her self-pity in an unusual project. For many years she has watched the newspapers in her city and has written comforting notes to parents who have lost a child. Her deep faith in Christ and her compassion for those who sorrow have made her a real blessing to many, many persons. Letters from parents who have been helped by her thoughtfulness bear its testimony.

One meeting her for the first time said: "I think your enjoyment in living is remarkable."

Quick came the answer, "Nonsense. It is just good common sense. I accepted my limitations and then got busy making the most of what I have."

Very wisely she balanced her interests. Scrabble, a word game, challenged her and she became a star player. Music and television added to her pleasures.

By all means be sure that you have invested in determination and courage. It takes determination to make this new assignment in living a glorious climax to the years that have passed. It takes real courage to carry it through to victory.

Remember, when the day seems dreary and loneliness haunts you, that there were such days in the past. Every heart knows these feelings. They are common to all.

Never say upon awakening, "How can I fill the long, dragging hours before me?" They are precious hours entrusted to you for wise use. An account must someday be given for their waste or misuse. It will help if you ask each morning upon awaking, "Lord Jesus, You have given to me a new day. Help me to forget the natural feelings of my heart. Show me how to fill it with cheerful thoughts and service."

Remember always, no day spent in fellowship with Christ can ever be called dreary.

Humor — an interest in others — the gift of appreciation — good common sense — determination and courage. These you will need if retirement years are to be enriching ones. One thing more, and this above all others — an unwavering faith in Christ and an unbroken confidence in the loving watchcare of your heavenly Father.

In His will is our peace.

Chapter 9

Don't Try So Hard

Sooner or later the retired woman will hear a persistent tapping at the door of her mind. With a little shiver of apprehension she may open it slightly to see the caller. And, in that waiting second, she meets a foe that she must conquer, or be conquered by it. It is called retirement panic. Backgrounds and circumstances influence each woman's reaction to this problem. But how to successfully meet this new way of living is the common need of the lonely woman.

Two friends of mine faced their first months of retirement at the same time. Charming women, unlike in personalities and backgrounds, they shared a common purpose — each was determined to make this new assignment in living a success.

Flora Swenson had recently been widowed. She had worked for many years with her husband. They had had no children and she now reluctantly sold her country home and moved into a town apartment. She had a bright, friendly manner and her light chitchat was amusing. Flora was invited to attend a large church.

The services were helpful but she felt lost in the congregation and homesick for the small church she had left.

In spite of all her good resolutions to make a good life, her spirits fell lower and lower. Finally the effort to go out, whether to church or to shop, became too great. In a few months Flora Swenson, a nervous, distraught woman, faced her doctor in his office.

"Mrs. Swenson," he told her, "you are ruining your health and you are doing it to yourself. You have substituted a healthy acceptance of being alone for a brooding, morbid longing for the past that can never be brought back.

"What is it costing you? Loss of your health and an apathy toward making new friends, finding new interests, or participating in any activities.

"I prescribe work for you — plain, everyday work. Find a simple part-time job and turn it into helpful therapy. Set your goal — one new friend within the month. And one project that you can share with others. It may be a church, civic, or club activity — whatever you choose. Try it and see me in a month."

Flora Swenson took her doctor's advice. Close to her home she found a friendly neighborhood church. She joined a class in the Sunday school that was made up of women alone even as she was. They invited her to join the group that went for dinner together each Sunday. The women's missionary circle became her project and she really enjoyed both its study group and work projects. And she found work. An elementary school cafeteria needed workers to serve the noonday lunch to its pupils. Mrs. Swenson was accepted and for a few hours each day she shared the noisy clamor of lively boys and girls.

Is Flora Swenson a happy woman now? Perhaps not

if measured by the years of companionship she shared in the old life. Perhaps not by comparison to her first choices and desires. But measured by a mature acceptance of changed circumstances and bolstered by her courage and effort, Flora Swenson has found a peaceful heart. Isn't that a priceless possession?

Alice Derrick had a professional background. Successful for years in her work, her time had been completely filled. Retirement faced her as an enemy, a foe about to destroy her well-ordered life. Immediately she turned her energy toward filling each day with commitments.

With admiration I watched her absorbed in many, many interests. Then I watched her with a question growing in my mind. What did all this hectic activity really tell? Was it the satisfaction of sharing and contributing? Was she in reality giving substantial help to each? Then one day I learned the answer. Quite frankly we were discussing retirement and the professional woman.

"Retirement found me unwilling to relinquish my busy schedule," she told me. "I couldn't stand the thought of dropping out and allowing others to do my work. Physically I was weary, but mentally I clung to the prestige I had enjoyed. I liked to hear people say, 'Capable Alice Derrick, a brilliant leader.'

"Almost frantically I joined study groups, book clubs, civic projects, and held offices in several organizations. I bought season tickets to all concerts and plays. I joined two bridge clubs."

She smiled wryly. "I've gone to sleep in a study group. I have dozed through book reviews. Some of the activities bore me. But I have been afraid to refuse any invitation given to me. I can't stand the thought of being left out or of being inactive. The thought of it fills me with terror."

Alice Derrick was making the mistake that many others do. It is possible to spread one's self so thin that really little is accomplished in any endeavor. I wanted to say to her, "Please don't try so hard. Choose those activities that appeal to your true interests and give them your best. But stop being so afraid of being alone with yourself; that can be a pleasant experience, too."

Once more we realize that there is no tried and proved way to turn loneliness into a happy, enjoyable experience. Perhaps it is small comfort to remember that no heart forever escapes pain. The poet said:

> Be still, sad heart! And cease repining;
> Behind the clouds is the sun still shining;
> Thy fate is the common fate of all,
> Into each life some rain must fall,
> Some days must be dark and dreary.

There are days when to be really cheerful, or at a moment's notice to turn a sunny smile to the world, is almost impossible. But to center one's thoughts on the blessings received daily is to develop a very wise habit. It is a habit that will safeguard us against the loneliest of moods.

Retirement years offer a special gift. It is a valuable and precious gift. In the busy, crowded years one caught fleeting glimpses of wonderful things that could be done if only one possessed it. Elusive daydreams wove fanciful tales of one day making these wishful dreams come true. God in His wisdom has measured out to each man, woman, boy, and girl an allotted amount of this gift. To some He gives more than to others. But from every living soul God will call for a report of the use made of His gift. It is not to be wasted; not to be frantically clung to; not to be overcrowded with meaningless things. We call it *time*.

"If only I had the time," we have sighed in our busy, active days. "There are so many things I want to do."

"Time passes so slowly," we whine when active schedules are relaxed. "What can I do with the time that hangs so heavily on my hands?"

What can you do? So close that you can reach out and touch them are many interesting things waiting for you. Simple, everyday things, some of them. Things that can easily be overlooked. They offer a sense of receiving that far outweighs the effort made to use them. They can relax taut nerves and stimulate jaded minds with the tingle of challenge.

Think of having time to think! That is a word not often used today. Youth is inclined to smile indulgently or even with a flicker of disdain at its old-fashioned sound. Nevertheless, it is a good word, a telling word — *muse*. It is the art of quiet meditation. God knew its value and He advises us in His Word to practice its use.

"Whatsoever things are true, whatsoever things are honest, whatsoever things are just, whatsoever things are pure, whatsoever things are lovely, whatsoever things are of good report; if there be any virtue, and if there be any praise, think on these things" (Philippians 4:8).

Quiet thinking is healing and strength-renewing. Webster defines the word *virtue* as a "beneficial quality or power of a thing." Thinking that lifts us above our personal needs and centers our thoughts on the truly worthwhile things of life is of great virtue. On the negative side, thoughts that dwell upon personal hurts or painful memories, have the power to deplete strength and to depress. Remember the prayer of David? "Let the words of my mouth and the meditation of my heart, be acceptable in thy sight, O Lord, my strength and my redeemer" (Psalm 19:14).

There is another word that is very popular in this day. Add one letter and in the place of *muse* you have *amuse*. Turn the dial on your television set and you have instant entertainment. Television has brought the world close to us. It provides current information as well as interesting programs and light amusement. But isn't it a pity if one allows activities or entertainment to crowd out the most important things? Especially those that give to us a serenity of spirit?

Who hasn't promised herself that some day when she has more time she will read to her heart's content? Well, now is the time to keep that promise to yourself. But it is unlikely to happen unless it is given planned time on the day's schedule. Such moments have a way of getting lost in aimless chatter or just plain procrastination.

One short half hour set aside for worthwhile reading brings surprising results. Not only is the mind stirred by fresh ideas but one's conversation becomes more interesting to others. Good reading broadens the understanding. It provokes thinking and encourages personal opinions and convictions.

A good book is like a visit from a wise friend who shares with you the wealth of his experience. You are always a richer person for the sharing. Everyone needs good book-friends. The mental pleasure they give is exhaustless.

From the Greeks came the old saying, "Books are

the medicine of the soul." Whatever the mood or the interest there is a book to meet it. Suppose you have never been an avid reader. It is not too late to cultivate a new habit, particularly such a good one. Try it and see.

Some of us have smiled over the homey philosophy of Mrs. Wiggs of the Cabbage Patch. With her special cheerfulness she advised:

> I jes do the best I ken where the good Lord put me at, an it looks like I got a happy feeling in me 'most all the time.

Remember her words to Lovey Mary?

> Don't you go and git sorry for yerself. That's one thing I can't stand in nobody. There's always lots of other folks you kin be sorry fer 'stid of yerself. Ain't you proud you ain't got a harelip? Why, that one thought is enough to keep me from ever gittin' sorry for myself.

We read the words, smile — and promptly turn to our own thoughts. But those wise words point like arrows in the right direction. There really can be no satisfying days if there is no time given to others. Boredom can become a chronic disease and its antidote is service.

In a large, attractive home in the suburbs of an eastern city Beth Eldon lived alone after the death of her parents. An only child, she had inherited a modest annual income. Life had been pleasant for Beth. She shared the Christian faith of her parents and now she sought to find an outlet in service.

"What can I do," she wondered. "I am not trained for either the professional or business world. My whole life has been spent in this home."

Soon after, her doctor told her about a patient that he had in the city.

"She needs to get away from the heat and noise," he told her. "She has been ill and two weeks of quiet rest would give her an opportunity to recover her strength."

"I have only my home," Beth told him, "but I will gladly share it with guests who have special needs."

That was the beginning of a unique service. Beth's guest book became her treasure book. It held the names of house guests — home and foreign missionaries, many other Christian workers, nurses, young businesswomen, underprivileged children, sick mothers, and many weary and discouraged strangers.

"I simply made use of what I had," Beth told a friend. "I have accepted the guests that Christ sent me and cared for them in His name. I have learned that those who needed me have been the ones that I most needed. Each guest has brought a special blessing to my life. I feared loneliness. He sent strangers who became dear friends. I dreaded hours of idleness. He filled the days with pleasant tasks. What one gives for Christ he receives doubly in return."

To the woman who loves the house of God her church can offer very promising opportunities for service. Missionary circles appeal especially to the woman who enjoys projects, needle craft, and handwork. Visitation work is a real ministry.

Hildred Evans was lonely but far too shy to venture out among strangers. She first visited a missionary circle as the guest of a neighbor. Before long she became a regular member and found her own special work.

A gift for letter writing was discovered in this timid, reserved woman. That warmth of friendly interest that she was too shy to show, was felt in her writing. She became missionary secretary.

Missionaries from many lands looked forward to her letters with their newsy bits from their home church. Their birthdays were always remembered by Hildred Evans and Christmas always brought a letter. Mission fields became real places to her. She studied these countries and learned about the cultures and their customs. Her prayer life expanded to include the needs of the missionaries. In this simple service a lonely woman found that the way to happiness lies in living for others.

Jane Devan was a unique character. She had never married and had worked in the credit department in a large store for many years. She was an odd looking Pied Piper but her deep love for children drew them to her wherever she went. Black or white, clean or dirty, it made no difference to this woman — she loved them all. She took retirement in her stride and calmly set about making the most of this newly acquired wealth — time. Everyone called her Miss D. For years she had lived in probably the most modest house on a very modest street.

Soon word reached the children that all were invited to Miss D's home for a weekly story hour. One story hour grew into others; spread to underprivileged neighborhoods; to children's hospital wards; to summer park programs. Miss D knew how to tell stories that made young hearts and minds respond to the good, the pure, and the right.

Some may have thought of Miss D as a rather nondescript sort of person with limited means and ability. How wrong they were. Miss D had learned that happiness can be found anywhere if its spring is in one's own heart.

Hospital auxiliaries invite the older woman with leisure time to give volunteer service in our often understaffed hospitals. Many convalescent homes are in need of women to visit their lonely shut-ins. To read them a comforting passage from God's Word, or to write the letter that trembling hands are not able to write may seem like unimportant things. But when they are done in His name, they take on new meaning and purpose.

Interested in studying French cooking? Creative writing? Fun with words? Philosohy? Spanish? Sewing? Interior decorating? Antiques?

Too late for that? Indeed, it isn't. Now you have time for this adventure. Adult education has opened up a whole new world for the older person. Now there is time to study and to share discussions with others of similar interests.

Retirees in college towns are particularly fortunate, for most colleges today offer day and evening courses for adults who wish to return to the classroom. Other cities and towns offer similar night courses through the public school facilities.

That is part of the joy of living — one need never stop learning. Our minds were never intended to hibernate at sixty-five. We are told to redeem the time and to invest it wisely.

Begin each morning with anticipation. Not with the eagerness of youth, perhaps, but not with panic for the fleeting years. Anticipation must be followed by participation, being part of the world about us.

All work and no play makes Jill a dull woman. Relaxation is needed for balance. What is enjoyable to one may be boring to another. The thought of a hobby may appeal to one woman and leave another indifferent. Whatever you enjoy most is right for you.

One shut-in learned that many missionaries can use old Christmas card covers in their work. She found real pleasure in collecting, trimming, and sending them around the world. The acknowledgments that she received from the missionaries sparked an interest in foreign stamps. This invalid became an expert stamp collector.

Two lively, young grandsons were responsible for one grandmother's involvement in a coin collection. It became her favorite hobby.

Whatever the individual interests, one thing is important to remember. Time must be balanced lest it become lopsided. Don't try so hard to fill the hours that selection plays no part.

"Hold out your hands," God says. "See, I give you golden hours to spend. You can make them glow with beauty or tarnish them with wastefulness. The choice is yours."

Surely each one should honor Him by giving back to Him precious time spent in prayer and reading His Word. Nothing can start the day as beautifully as a "Good Morning" prayer. Nothing can close the day as peacefully as a "Thank You" prayer for His protection and goodness. And nothing in all the world can calm upset nerves or renew strength like taking time to talk things over with Him during the day.

Last years may be the best of all, for hearts are wiser and many lessons have been learned. Don't try so hard to fill the hours but try persistently to live each day with heart rest and purpose.

Faults are thick when love is thin.

Chapter 10

Elastic Tape Measures

It is easy to set up the ideal pattern of conduct for others. Family living has a way of developing tolerance of family faults and bad habits. They may be irritating but the sense of family loyalty forbids discussing them with outsiders. Unfortunately that attitude doesn't always extend to those outside the family circle. Living alone sometimes has the tendency to narrow one's tolerance and understanding of imperfections seen in others.

Nettie Brown was the village dressmaker. A perky, grey-haired little woman, her dark eyes sparkled with enthusiasm. Nettie Brown really enjoyed her work and people.

"How are you able to fit your patrons so well?" she was asked.

"Maybe," the seamstress answered, "it's because I try to fit my pattern to the person instead of trying to make her fit the pattern."

Dress patterns come in all sizes — with perfect lines and measurements. Unfortunately few of us have perfect measurements. A pattern must be altered to cover a stoop, a lopsidedness or other physical defects.

People come in all sizes and shapes, too. And not one can measure up to perfection. Each of us has some small habit, personality trait, or mannerism that annoys someone else.

Try putting a bit of elastic in your measuring tape. You will be a much happier and less lonely woman. Possibilities of pleasant acquaintances or closer friendships can be overlooked if one sees only the small peculiarities. If a little tolerance is mixed with humor and good will, it has the power to stretch out insignificant kinks and reach from heart to heart.

Another's motive for an act is often misconstrued. What is clear and above reproach to the doer may be construed differently by the other. Here an elastic tape measure comes in handy. Stretch your willingness to give the benefit of the doubt. Fold up your judgment and put it away unused.

Jane Upton and Nelda Smith had been friends for many years. They worked in the same department and had many interests in common. As she grew older Nelda's tongue grew more caustic. Her criticisms became more cutting. When retirement notice was given it came to her as a personal injustice. Then she learned that Jane had said that it would have been better had Nelda retired earlier for she had failed physically the last few years. Immediately she turned against her old friend. Never has she believed that concern for her health prompted those words.

Foolish? Yes, isn't it. Yet isn't it usually small, insignificant things that grow into big hurts? The interesting thing was to watch how each woman used her measuring tape.

Nelda pulled hers tight and held it straight. Her friend had failed to measure up to her requirements.

Jane's feelings were hurt and she was miserable when her attempts to explain were refused. Then her sense of fairness came to her rescue.

"What I can't change, I must accept," she decided. "I will remember the good years and her many fine qualities. I will understand that physical problems have caused her to become as she is now."

Jane wasn't aware of it but the elastic in her measuring tape had stretched to fit with understanding a crippled friendship.

Jimmy was a friendly youngster, quick to make friends and slow to believe ill of any. It was a perfect day for sledding and Jimmy and his friends were enjoying it to the full. Coming down the hill Jimmy failed to stop in time and his sled caught in the dress of a lady crossing the street.

Frightened he looked up at her and said, "I'm sorry. I didn't see you in time."

She smiled down at him. "Never mind," she assured him, "no great damage is done. And accidents do happen, we know."

"But I tore your dress," the young boy told her. "I thought you would be angry."

"A torn dress can be mended, my dear," she said gently, "but angry words can't always be repaired."

Jimmy watched her as she crossed the street and went on her way.

"Isn't she beautiful?" he asked his friends.

"Who, that lady?" they laughed. "You must be blind. Why, she is old and her face is wrinkled."

Jimmy was silent for a moment, then he said as he pulled his sled back up the hill, "But I saw her soul and it was beautiful."

What Jimmy didn't see was her measuring tape. It

had stretched to excuse a small boy's clumsiness. But in the stretching a memory was born in the heart of a young boy. It was his for always. Jimmy never forgot the lovely lady who met a boy's fear of a reprimand with gentle forgiveness and understanding.

There is a great need for a special kind of elastic tape measure. It would have a big market if only it could be manufactured. However, the ones who need it most are usually the last to realize it. It should have a special label marked "For mothers of married daughters and sons."

Six qualities of character blended together are guaranteed to make an elastic tape measure that will lessen the emptiness in a lonely mother's heart. None are new. In fact, they are so old that we pass over them in searching for newer and more popular ones. Don't let their age deceive you. It is their strongest selling point — they have been tested and proven true. They claim no magic, only the power to help in difficult situations. The first four should be used in equal amounts, the last two should be doubled. They are, in proper order, acceptance, remembrance, enjoyment, praise, tact, and silence.

Acceptance. How many times we meet this word. It begins every successful assignment that God entrusts to us. It is around the corner of any change in our lives that He sees fit to make. It must head the list, for without it there is only chaos of emotions.

Accept that daughter-in-law, that son-in-law — not only in the expected conventional manner but in the heart. This is the initial step in establishing a good relationship. If the choice was not the one you most wanted, never put that disappointment into words.

Accept this new member in your family as he is, as

she is. Stretch your measuring tape to accept the personality traits, good or bad, the habits, the ways that differ from yours.

Remembrance. At times this can be a problem word that can be either a help or a hindrance. When tempted to remember only the virtues of your children, remember, too, their willful moments, the strong wills that wanted to make personal choices. Remembering can prod your common sense. Your child, you must acknowledge, was not perfect either.

Remembrance has another side. It can take a mother back to her first years as a bride. Forgotten feelings and incidents can be pulled out of the memory bag if the searching fingers are honest ones.

That desire to live independently of parents — to make mistakes, if necessary, without asking for advice — to establish a home that expresses individual tastes — to live as a separate, independent family — all these are reminders. They were your natural instincts, now you find them again in your children.

Enjoyment. Being a mother-in-law can be quite an education. It can be fun, too. One learns that holidays, birthdays, family dinners don't have to hold fast to family traditions. New families make new traditions. When you are invited, be an interesting guest who shows honest enjoyment and appreciation.

Christmas gifts come in an amazing assortment of wrappings. That elegant box covered with paper of shining gold with its bow of satin may wait unopened, while a wobbly bow tied by little hands takes the place of honor. It is the love that counts and the pure joy of being together. The *why* is so much more important than the *how*.

There are new ways and new touches that the older

woman can learn. They add attractiveness to the old ways. Young wives have a way of coming up with clever ideas. Enjoy being the learner.

Grandmothers have special lessons to learn. Elementary courses begin with that tousle-haired little grandson, that cuddly baby granddaughter. Advance lessons cover the school years to young adulthood. In fact, no grandmother ever really graduates. Learning is continuous. Lessons may vary but certain fundamentals carry through all the courses.

Usually the most difficult lesson to learn is the proper use of the measuring tape. The problem is to find the right amount of elastic. Strangely enough the lack of elasticity in measuring the parents is often in sharp contrast to the excess used in measuring those beloved grandchildren. A loving grandmother is a blessing. However, there are some warnings worth heeding.

Love for the grandchildren should be balanced by accepting the fact that their training is the responsibility of their parents. New methods will replace the ones that grandmother used. These decisions are not hers to make. She is very wise not to criticize or to offer unsolicited advice.

Enjoy your role in the family life. Give yourself generously to those youngsters who have brought you such pleasure. Then, add to that measuring tape enough elastic to give the young parents plenty of respect and encouragement for the stupendous task that is theirs. Enjoy their enjoyment, Grandmother.

Praise. Everyone responds to sincere praise. It is such a small thing to give and its power is surprisingly great. What can praise do? Many things.

Praise can turn discouragement into successful new efforts. It can lift weary hearts into feelings of exultation. It can turn indifference into warm friendships. Praise has the power to heal deep hurts. It strengthens family ties and nurtures appreciation in the heart of the giver. Praise does all this and more. Why, I wonder, are we so stingy with its use?

Praise for a daughter-in-law or a daughter's husband can leave a gentle, beneficial touch. It may bring as much pleasure as a bouquet of red roses. Praise closes its eyes to an untidy house and a small child's dirty face. It speaks only of the bright eyes and happy smile.

Praise notices the splendid efforts of the breadwinner but never mentions his faults. Praise admires the attractive purchase with no censure for the extravagance. Praise sees fine qualities but omits criticisms.

Praise can mend bruises and put a lilt in a heart. But it must be honest praise, heartfelt. Examine that tape measure. Plenty of praise in the elastic? Use it freely; you can't exhaust the supply.

Tact. We were taught that politeness is to do and say the kindest thing in the kindest way. What is tact? It is the ability to say or do that which will maintain good relations and avoid offense. Tactfulness oils the machinery of family relations and keeps it running smoothly.

"She is so tactless," we hear someone say of another. Perhaps this woman may never develop this quality into a polished grace but honest effort can help wonderfully.

Where is tact needed more than in family relationships? In daily associations nerves can be rubbed the wrong way and irritations build up. Because the mother-in-law is older and more experienced in family living it is important for her to be wisely tactful.

"It's getting late," said Bill to his young wife. "Let's go."

Turning to his wife's mother he said in leaving, "Sorry we stayed so long. Didn't realize that program on TV would last so long."

"Well," came the tactless answer, "to tell the truth we were tired and planned to go to bed early. We don't care for that program."

To himself Bill added, "It won't happen again."

Couldn't she have said, "You are always welcome. I am glad that you enjoyed the program"?

It pays to think before words are spoken. It is so easy to unintentionally offend another. Sometimes silence is the most tactful answer of all. Practice using tact; never be without it.

Silence. "Silence is golden," says the old quote. But there are times that silence can be condemning. At other times it gives apparent consent to something inwardly unwanted. But the ability to be silent at the right moment is an art worth cultivating.

A quiet smile with no words spoken can answer a barbed remark and leave no sting. Silence with gentleness makes petty behavior seem childish. And to be silent — when angry, cutting words scream to be spoken — is the wisest silence of all.

Silence is the mother-in-law's best ally. It keeps her safely out of decisions and problems that should be settled between the young couple. It is her protection when spoken words would erect barriers. Consequently, it is the surest way to win and keep the respect of her family.

When a mother learns to stand quietly by, ready to help if needed, and to remain silent when words ought not to be spoken, she has mastered the use of the elastic tape measure.

We have talked much about love. Christ came to teach us its power. God's love for sinful man. Christ's saving love toward us. Our love first for Him then reaching out to others for His sake. This is love in its purest form. It is a transforming love, an empowering love, a motivating love.

Christ told us, "I give you a new commandment, that you should love one another; just as I have loved you, so you, too, should love one another" (John 13:34).

Love that comes from loving Christ is a love that blesses others. But sometimes it is difficult to love one whom you find unlovely.

"How can I love this person?" asked a young Christian facing this problem.

A wise teacher gave this answer, "Practice seeing that person, not as he is now, but as he will be if Christ wins his heart."

It will help you, try it and see.

The story of Angeline Tucker tells of a love for Christ that triumphed over tragedy and heartbreak. It is told in her book, *He Is in Heaven.* I know Angeline, she is my friend. A Christian woman whose love for Christ answered the call to the mission field. A frail woman with strong courage. A wife who shared her husband's missionary vision and worked gladly by his side in Congoland. A mother who covered her three children with her unshaken faith when tragedy came.

Paulus, a city in northeast Congo, became the home of the J. W. Tuckers. Twenty-five years of missionary service put down deep roots of love for this people. Here was the new church where Congolese Christians came to worship. Here was their work, their plans, their hopes.

Following their declared state of independence Congo became a land of unrest and rebellion. Tense fear paralyzed the people. Closer and closer it came to Paulus. Then, suddenly, raging, hate-crazed Simbas filled the city, ravaging and destroying.

Drugged with dope and hatred they took the white missionary away as Angeline and their children watched helplessly. Gathering them close Angeline led her little family in prayer. They prayed for their father's safety and for God's watchcare over them. They asked for courage not to be afraid but to be strong and trust in God's unfailing love.

Days of terror followed. J. W. Tucker was released to return to his family only to again be taken prisoner. On November 24, 1964, J. W. Tucker gave his life for the people he had come to love. Rescued by American paratroopers Angeline Tucker and her children were flown home to the States.

Accepting with quiet dignity her new assignment in living Angeline has daily lived the truths that she taught. There is no room in her heart for bitterness or self-pity. She is making a normal, happy life for her children while she is working in the missions department of her denomination. Her loneliness and heartbreak have been channeled into service to others.

Angeline Tucker has learned the meaning of love. The need of Congoland is the need on her heart. Her love for the Congolese Christians stretches out to gather in the rebelling Simbas, murderers of the white missionary who came only to tell them of God's love.

She is one of countless lonely women in our land today. But she is proving by her life that Christ's grace is sufficient. And she is showing us that the best cure for loneliness is reaching out to help others.

Christian character is not an inheritance; each individual must build it for himself.

— UNKNOWN

Chapter 11

Spiritual Pickups

When a mother has to leave her family for a time she leaves all kinds of instructions. What to do — what not to do. Where to find needed articles — what to eat — what to wear — hours to keep — whom to call in case of emergency. This list is long but it speaks of love. It shows love for her family and concern for its needs.

As the time drew near for Christ to return to heaven, He was concerned for His children. Often He talked with His disciples, preparing them for His absence. Christ gave His promise that one day He will return for those who belong to Him. And He did not leave us unprotected. He gave us God's Word. It contains His promise to guide us, protect us, and keep us. Nothing can touch a Christian's life that His Word does not cover. But it must be read with faith, acted upon with confidence.

All the varying moods and experiences that make up the everydayness of our lives are found in the Bible. Problems common to us all are listed. Solutions are given, also.

101

In this last chapter may I share with you some of the helps that are found in God's Word for us?

Eventide Prayer

And when Aaron lighteth the lamps at even, he shall burn a perpetual incense before the Lord.
— Exodus 30:8

Eventide — soft darkness — rest from the day's work — loneliness for loved ones — memories — the backward glance at the day's story — the lighting of the lamp of prayer — the blessed release of sleep.

The very word "eventide" stirs thoughts of peace and rest. Today may have been difficult for you. That problem may have been wearing and the clamor of tensions unbearable. Then this is for you.

When the evening lamps were lighted, incense was burned upon the altar. Its fragrance rose as an acceptable sacrifice before the Lord. The altar of incense speaks to us of prayer.

"Come," says Christ. "If you are weary, come and find rest. If you are troubled I will give you peace. If weak, I will give you strength. If you are afraid I will give you courage."

It is yours for the asking. Like a weary child, light the lamp of prayer at the close of the day. Then, in simple childlike faith relinquish your tired, jangled nerves into the healing hands of the Lord Jesus. Relax in His care. The fragrance of your faith honors Him and He honors your faith.

A Morning Faith

When you wake up in the morning
'Ere you tread the untried day
Of the path that lies before you,

In the coming busy day;
Whether sunbeams promise gladness,
Whether dark forbodings fall;
Be your dawning glad or gloomy,
Go in prayer and tell Him all.
                    — Author Unknown

The Place of Safety

The beloved of the Lord shall dwell in safety
by him; and the Lord shall cover him all day
long, and he shall dwell between his shoulders.
                    — Deuteronomy 33:12

One day I read these words and wondered about
their meaning. Somehow I felt that they held a precious truth if only I could understand it. It was many
years later that I found the explanation. Now this
verse is marked "special" in my Bible.

We lose some very precious truths because the western mind is unused to the manners and customs of the
Bible lands. The meaning of this verse was very clear
to the Old Testament woman.

With the rising of the eastern sun the family arose
and the day's work began. Farmers lived in villages
for common protection from nomadic foes. Early in
the day they went out to the fields to work until sun-
down. Not only did the tent and village mothers care
for their households but they went out to work in the
fields.

In a small camel hair cradle, made by her hands,
the mother carried her baby between her shoulders.
It was held fast by strong cords across her forehead.
As she walked the rocky paths the baby looked con-
tentedly about, safe in his cradle. When the sun grew
warmer the mother carefully covered her baby with her

large white veil protecting it from the heat and insects. In the field the mother hung her baby's cradle on a low limb of a nearby tree where she could watch as she worked.

What is God telling us? That we are safe in His care. Always in God's Word the word *shoulder* is symbolic of strength. God's love is greater than a mother's love. Carefully with His divine strength He carries us in perfect safety through every day of our lives.

I thought of the baby in the cradle. Could it have spoken would it have said, "Watch out, Mother, the way is stony. If you lose your footing I will be hurt"?

Would it have cried out, "Are you sure that you know the way, Mother? You have come to a new field today. The way is strange"?

Foolish thinking, but doesn't it sound a bit familiar?

"The way is hard, Lord," we plead. "I feel so frightened, so unsure. Why, Lord, are you bringing me along this path?"

And all the while God is showing us that we are completely safe in His love. He not only knows the way before us but He chose the way. His way is the only safe way there is.

The small baby needed protection from the pestering insects that gathered around him. What of the small vexations that upset us? Some of us bear the bigger trials more victoriously than the small annoyances. Our heavenly Father is aware of our weaknesses. He has made provision for us. No matter what the day brings to a Christian there is a place of safety in God.

Advertising Christ

O magnify the Lord with me and let us exalt his name together.　　　　　　— Psalm 34:3

A retired minister was asked to supply the pulpit in our church until a new pastor could be chosen. My new husband of three weeks very happily told the board of deacons that we would entertain him the first Sunday. I was horrified. A strange guest for Sunday dinner! I was still consulting five cookbooks to prepare each evening dinner.

Very kindly our guest overlooked my inexperienced attempt and soon we felt at ease. We lingered at the table enjoying anecdotes from the minister's years of service. Then he said: "Wouldn't you like to read a bit from God's Word?"

Turning to Psalm 34:3 he asked us to read it together.

"O magnify the Lord with me, and let us exalt his name together."

"What does the word *magnify* mean?" he asked us.

I ventured an answer — "To magnify means to enlarge, to increase in significance."

It was then that our Sunday turned into a day always to be remembered with appreciation and gratefulness. That seasoned man of God taught us a needed lesson from this verse.

"You are right in your definition," he told me. "But you are only partly right. In the original the word meant *to advertise.*"

"O advertise the Lord with me," the Psalmist urged. To advertise means to call attention by emphasizing desirable qualities so as to arouse desire in another to possess it.

Sobering thought, isn't it? A Christian is responsible for so exhibiting the character of Christ in his life that others will seek the same spiritual experience. And the lonely Christian woman? Who can testify better than she to the blessings of living each day in fellowship with Christ?

To accept life's assignments with cheerful submission; to turn loneliness into joyful service; to meet disappointment without murmuring, to be gentle, forbearing, kind, patient in unpleasant situations — these are ways the heart finds to advertise Christ to others.

God's Reservoir

Thy God hath commanded thy strength.
— Psalm 68:28

Aunt Etta was such a comfort. She never seemed to live in the hectic rush that leaves most of us breathless. Quite content with her lot in life, Aunt Etta radiated cheerfulness. Her life had not always been easy. Sorrow had visited and sickness had often knocked at her door. But if you had a problem, then Aunt Etta was the right one to listen and to help.

It was she who told me about her favorite verse in the Psalms. She said, "When your supply of strength seems to be depleted and doesn't match the tasks facing you, don't be discouraged. If you do, what strength you have, either physical or spiritual will ooze away.

"Just close your eyes. Relax and recall the largest reservoir that you have ever seen. Did it store water to meet the town's need should there be a shortage emergency? Now picture in your mind a reservoir as high as the heavens, as broad as the sky. And then you have only begun to visualize God's reservoir of strength.

"Bible translators tell us that the word *reserved* gives a truer meaning than the word *commanded*. This means that sufficient strength is set apart by God to meet the need of every child of His. Your supply is

106

there waiting. As it is needed it is yours for the asking and taking.

" 'Thy God hath reserved strength for you.' "

As Aunt Etta says, "Isn't it hard to understand why Christians so often fail to take what is there waiting for them?"

Examination Time

O Lord, thou has searched me, and known me.
— Psalm 139:1

Many years have passed since I cut the following lines from a newspaper. Now they are yellowed with time and have become brittle to the touch. But they are as meaningful to me today as when I first read them.

Whenever I read them over I get the same feeling I experienced when it was exam time in school — particularly when the subject was math. Honest examination of my heart has never rated me a high grade. But the challenge is there and the desire to measure up grows stronger as I grow older.

May I share them with you?

Your Inner Self

I am the result of all that you have done and thought and felt. When you hated, that hate became part of you. When you shirked your task, that shirking became part of you. When you lusted, that unholiness became a part of you. When you loved and hoped, those graces entered into your inner self. When you faced the world in a courageous spirit, that courage helped to furnish your inner self. When you chose the generous and unselfish path, that self-forgetfulness entered into your inner self.

I am the inner destiny that decided what all else is to mean to you. When friendships are offered you; when books invite you; when pictures allure you; when tasks challenge you; when the future commands you — these become dead, or full of meaning and beauty, according to what I have become.

I am the sum total of your past added to the new impulses and acts of the present. I am the final executive officer who settles all the disputed questions of your day-by-day conduct.

I am your inner self.

— Author Unknown

A Blessing in Disguise

A faithful man shall abound with blessings.
— Proverbs 28:20

It was New Year's Eve. Like an aged monarch the old year stood in silent dignity as his young successor took the throne. I sat alone with my thoughts. They turned to the old year that had passed so quickly.

"It has been a good year," I thought, "I have much for which to be thankful."

Words from an old Sunday school hymn began to sing in my heart:

Count your blessings. Name them one by one,
Count your many blessings, see what God hath
done.

I began to list my blessings. Love of my family — my church — friendships — work — health — interesting activities — happy experiences — travel. . . .

"What am I forgetting?" I asked myself. "The list doesn't seem complete."

"Haven't you forgotten those lessons that you learned through discipline?" that inner voice prompted.

I remembered the lessons, all right, only I had never thought of them as *blessings*. Now, looking back, I realized that they had taught me some valuable lessons in self-control. They had helped me, too, to be slower in my judgment of others. I added them to the list.

Still I felt that it was unfinished. Then, out of the old year's experiences came one marked, "failure." I had been so self-confident, so sure of my own ability that I had forgotten an important truth. A Christian's source of success lies in acknowledging his complete dependence upon God's help. Memory of my failure still brought the sting of defeat. Tonight I recognized it as a blessing in disguise. I put it first on my list of blessings.

Bells were ringing, whistles blowing. My list was now complete. I knelt to pray for I wanted to begin the new year with a "thank you" for every blessing. Especially, I wanted to thank Him for that blessing called "failure."

Three Tenses of Trust

But we trusted. . . . — Luke 24:21

Christ's heart must have been sad that day on the way to Emmaus. He listened to His disciples as they spoke of their grief and shattered hopes. Not recognizing their Lord, they poured out their disappointment to Him.

"We trusted," they explained. "We trusted that He was our Messiah, the hope of Israel. We have waited three days but we have heard nothing."

There is nothing sadder than to hear a Christian speak of his faith in the past tense. Faith and trust were all Christ asked of His disciples. When the test came they spoke of them only as in the past.

"What time I am afraid, I will trust in Thee" (Psalm 56:3).

This is what Christ asks of every Christian. Not merely in words but trust that is put to daily practice. Not only when things look bright but when the dark clouds cover the brightness. It is the testing time that proves the worth of the claim. Fear is common to us all but to be overcome by fear puts the Christian's trust to shame. Christ has promised to be our help; lack of trust is dishonoring to Him. Let a rugged, strong trust grow in your heart — a trust for the *now* — *today*.

". . . I will trust and not be afraid" (Isaiah 12:2).

This is trust in its purest form. Fear drives away trust but trust destroys fear. This is a trust that makes the future secure. Its foundation is strong for it is built on a past trust that proved Christ's Word to be true. It gives a serenity of spirit for the present, knowing that Christ is in charge of every detail in your life. It faces the future with confidence believing that Christ will work all things out for His honor and glory.

Fragrance of a Rose

. . . I am the Rose of Sharon. . . .
— Song of Solomon 2:1

Here I will dwell, for I have desired it.
— Psalm 132:14

An old Persian fable has given us a beautiful picture. A wanderer one day, weary from the burning sun, stopped to rest under a shady tree. Evening shadows awakened him and he hurried to find shelter for the night.

In a small, barren room he became increasingly aware of a sweet perfume. He searched but could not find the source. Yet the fragrance persisted.

"What are you? Where are you?" he demanded.

Then his hand touched his loose robe. A small piece of clay fell from its folds. Picking it up he found the answer. That rare odor came from the small piece of clay.

"I don't understand," the wanderer said, "you have the fragrance of a gem from Smarcand. You could be a precious spikenard or another costly merchandise. But you are only a piece of clay. From where, then, comes this wondrous perfume?"

"O Sir," came the answer, "I am but a lump of common clay. I claim no beauty of my own, no fragrance. I am but the lowliest of substances. This is my secret. I have been dwelling with a rose."

This is the beauty secret of any woman's life — to choose to dwell with the Rose of Sharon. Then the lowliest life becomes fragrant and lovely. Within her may be feelings of loneliness or longings for things withheld. But with Christ dwelling within her heart, that sweet essence of His Spirit permeates her heart and mind. There is no beauty like the life lived with the Rose of Sharon, the One altogether lovely.